WOODCARVING THE FEMALE HEAD

A step-by-step guide
with
GEORG KEILHOFER

Written by
Bud LaBranche

Designed by: Patricia Novak
Illustrations by: Rick Rowden
Photography by: Rick Hominuk

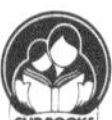

3312 MAINWAY, BURLINGTON, ONTARIO L7M 1A7, CANADA 2045 NIAGARA FALLS BLVD., UNIT 14, NIAGARA FALLS, NEW YORK 14304

To my good friend and mentor,
Bill Speirs
who stimulated my interest in woodcarving.

ISBN 0-88625-137-0

3312 MAINWAY, BURLINGTON, ONTARIO L7M 1A7, CANADA
2045 NIAGARA FALLS BLVD., UNIT 14,NIAGARA FALLS, NEW YORK 14304

Printed and bound in Canada
by
T. H. Best Printing Company Limited

FOREWORD

No matter how hard anyone tries to describe a carving procedure, it is impossible to cover every step. This book is designed as a guide to assist you in carving the female head.

SECTION 1

HOLDING DEVICES

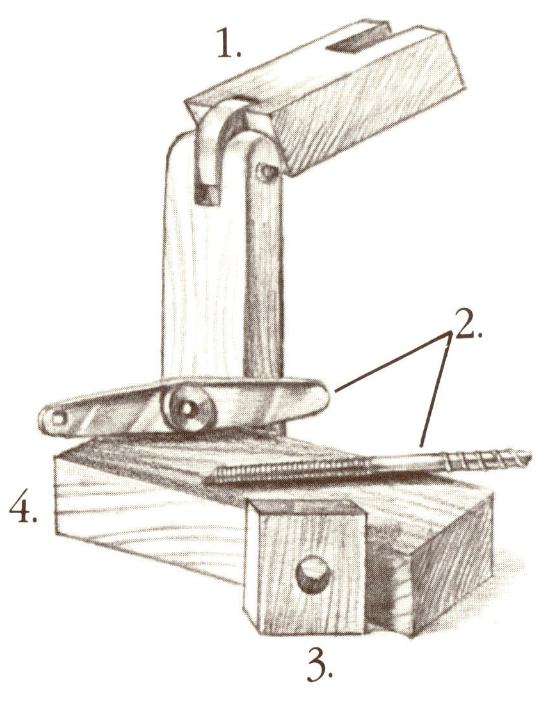

1. Carving arm
2. ⅜" carving screw
3. Hardwood spacer block
4. Basswood carving block

DIMENSIONS

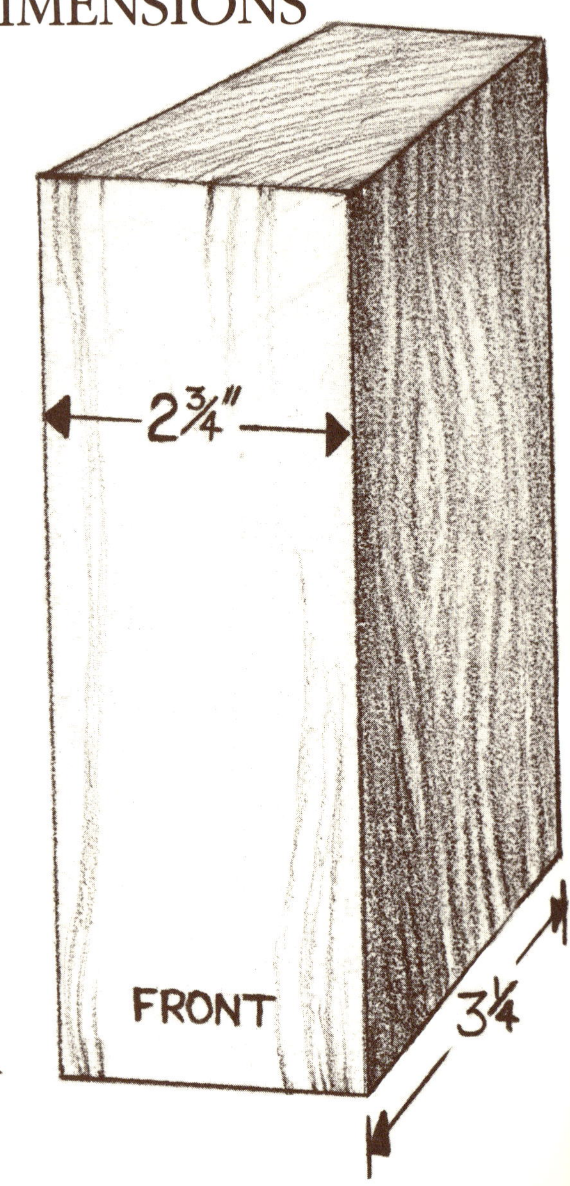

1. Using a ¼" gimlet, make a pilot hole 1 ½" deep in the center of the block of wood.

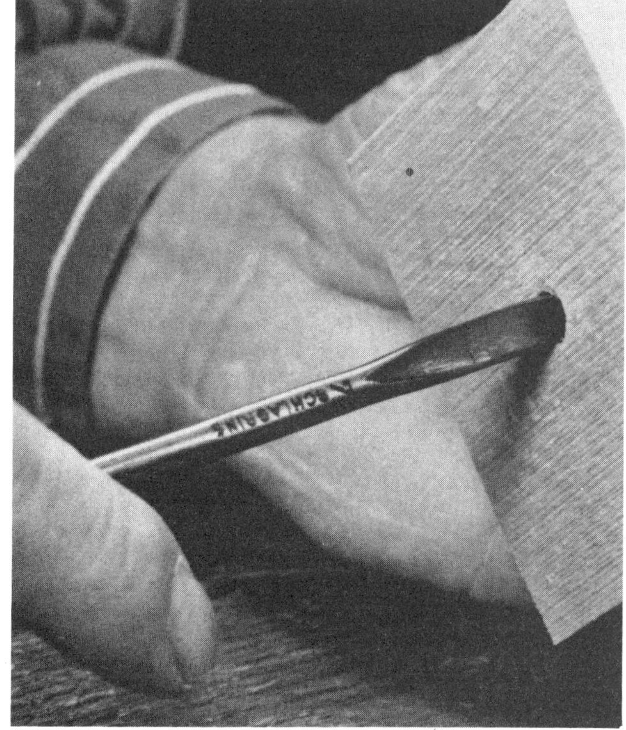

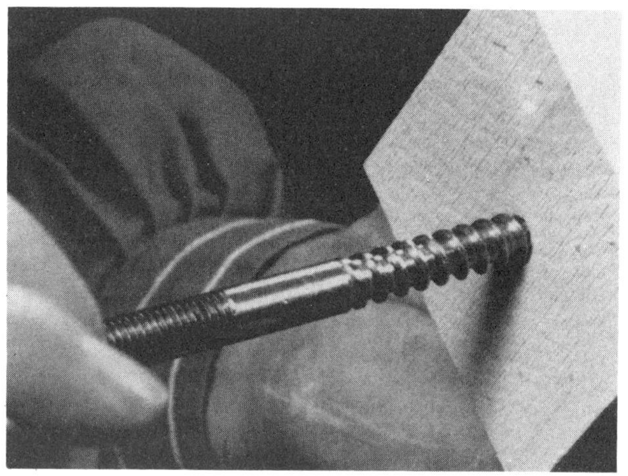

2. Insert the carving screw.

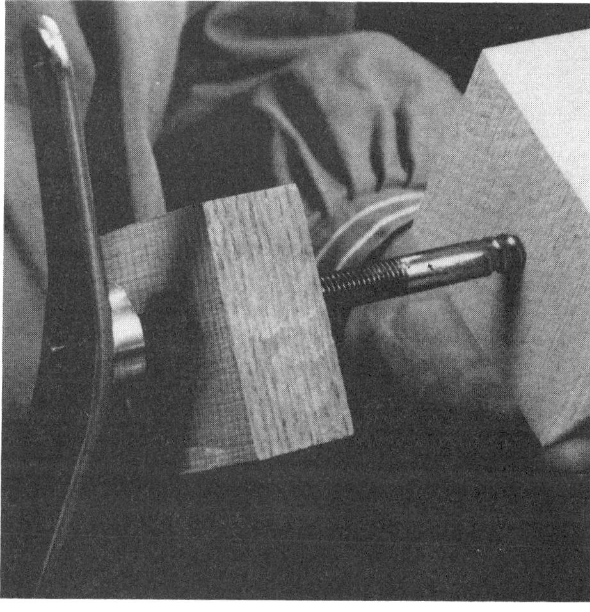

3. A hardwood spacer block will cut down on the wear of the carving arm.

4. Place the carving arm in the vice or clamp to the bench top. ➤

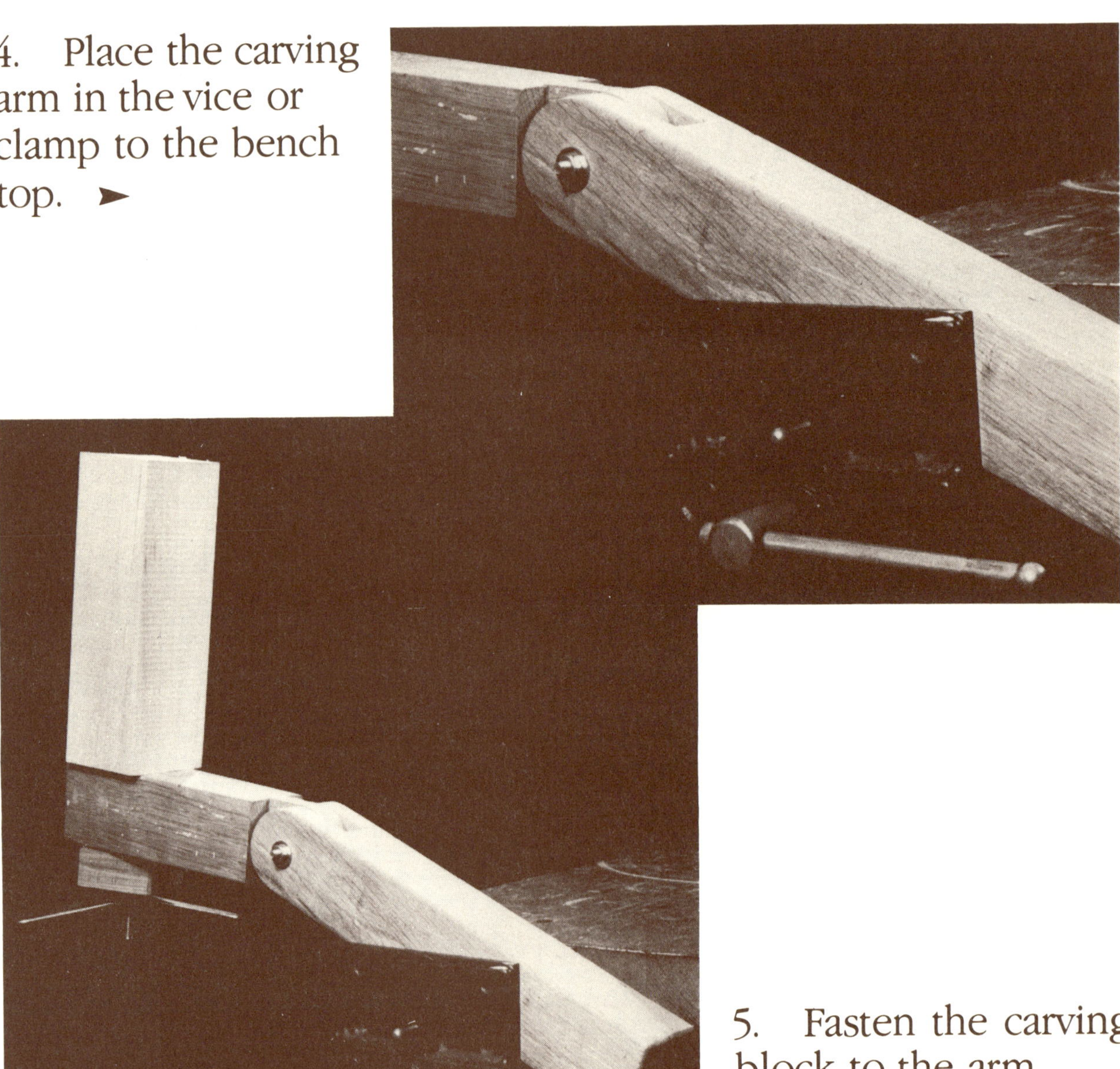

5. Fasten the carving block to the arm.

6. Measure down 2 ¾" from the top and draw a level line. This will create a square 2 ¾" x 2 ¾".

8. Draw a centered horizontal line.

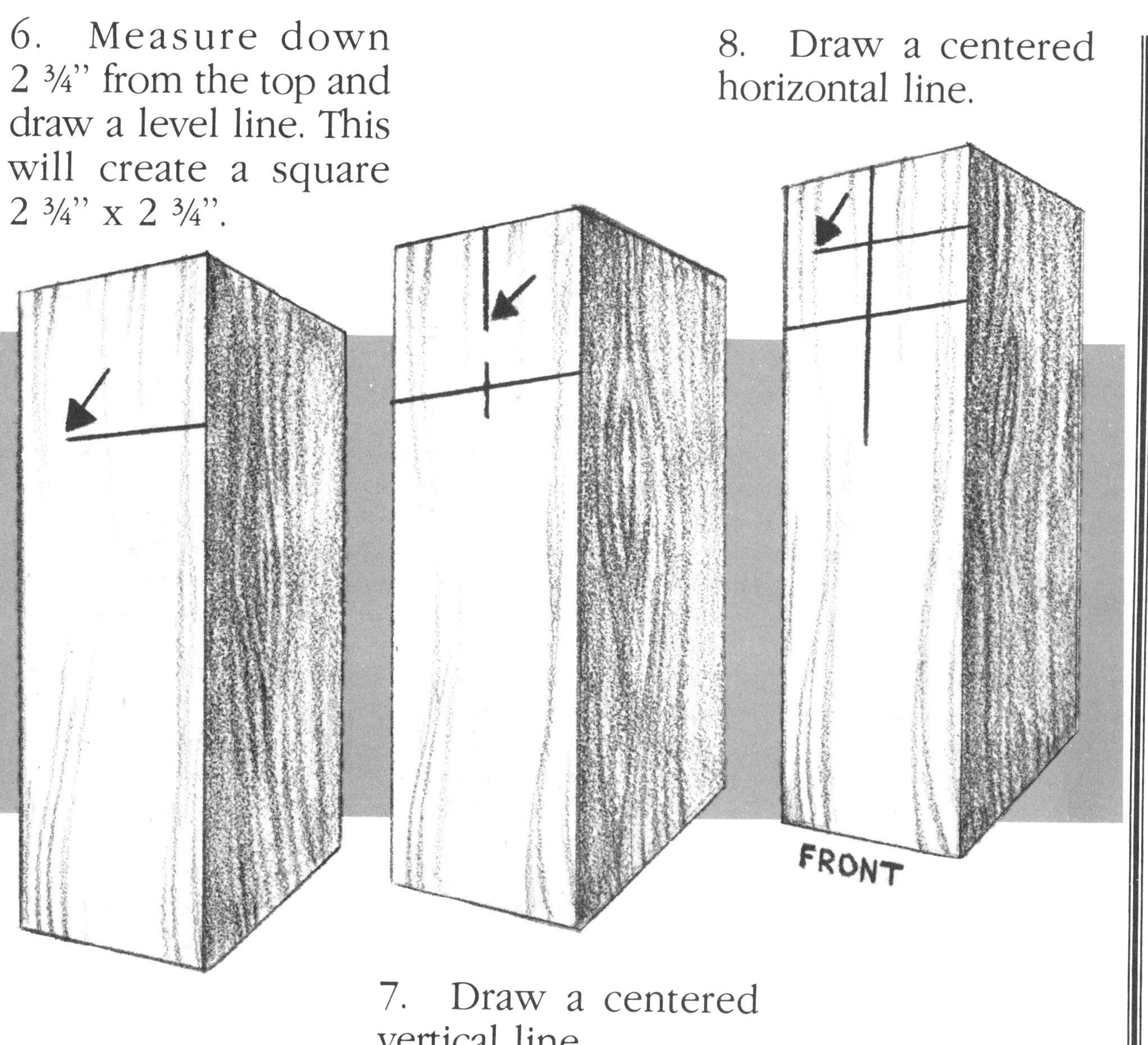

7. Draw a centered vertical line.

9. Find the center of the top and bottom halves. Find the center of the bottom half.

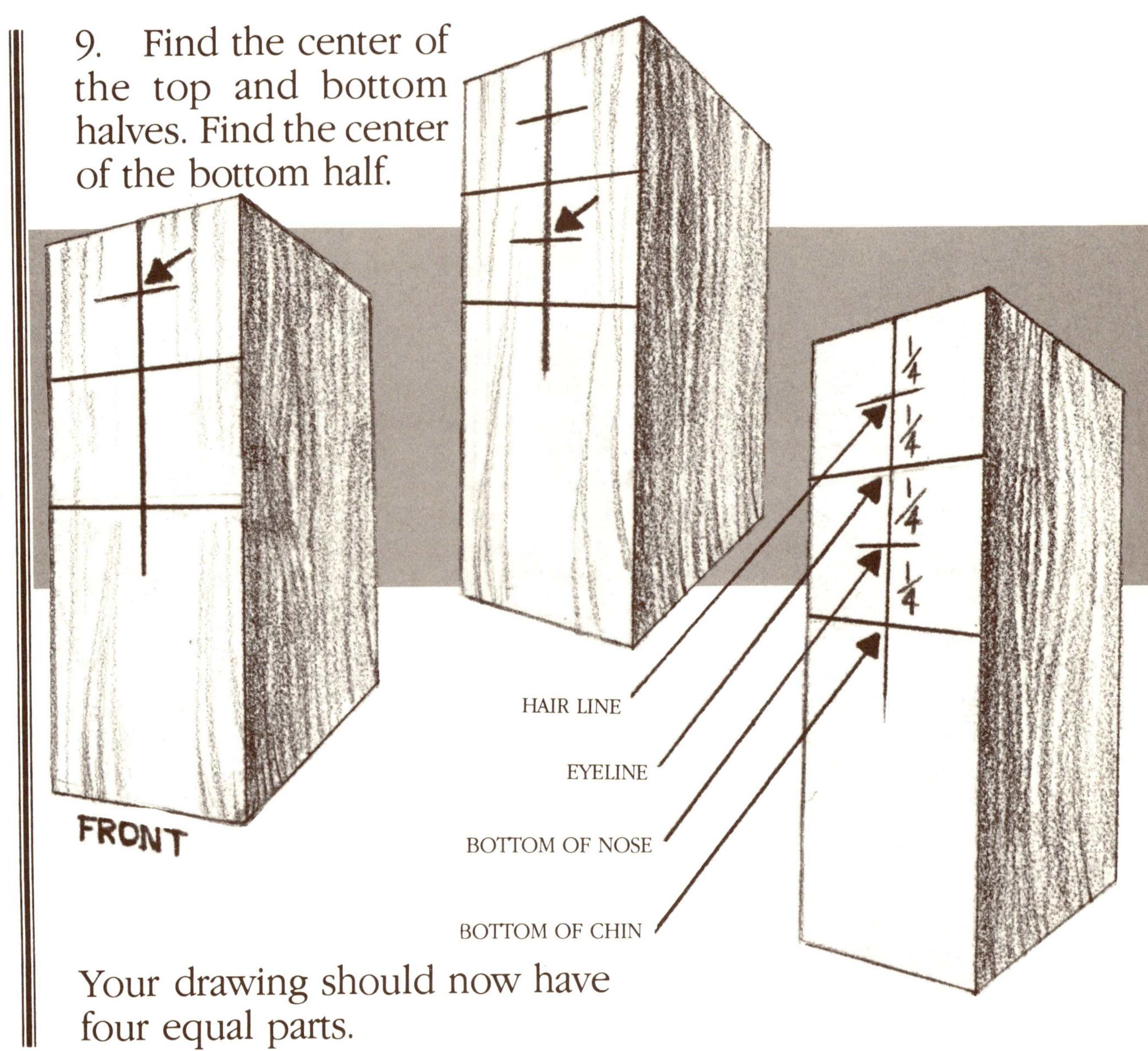

Your drawing should now have four equal parts.

10. Divide the front into six vertical equal parts.

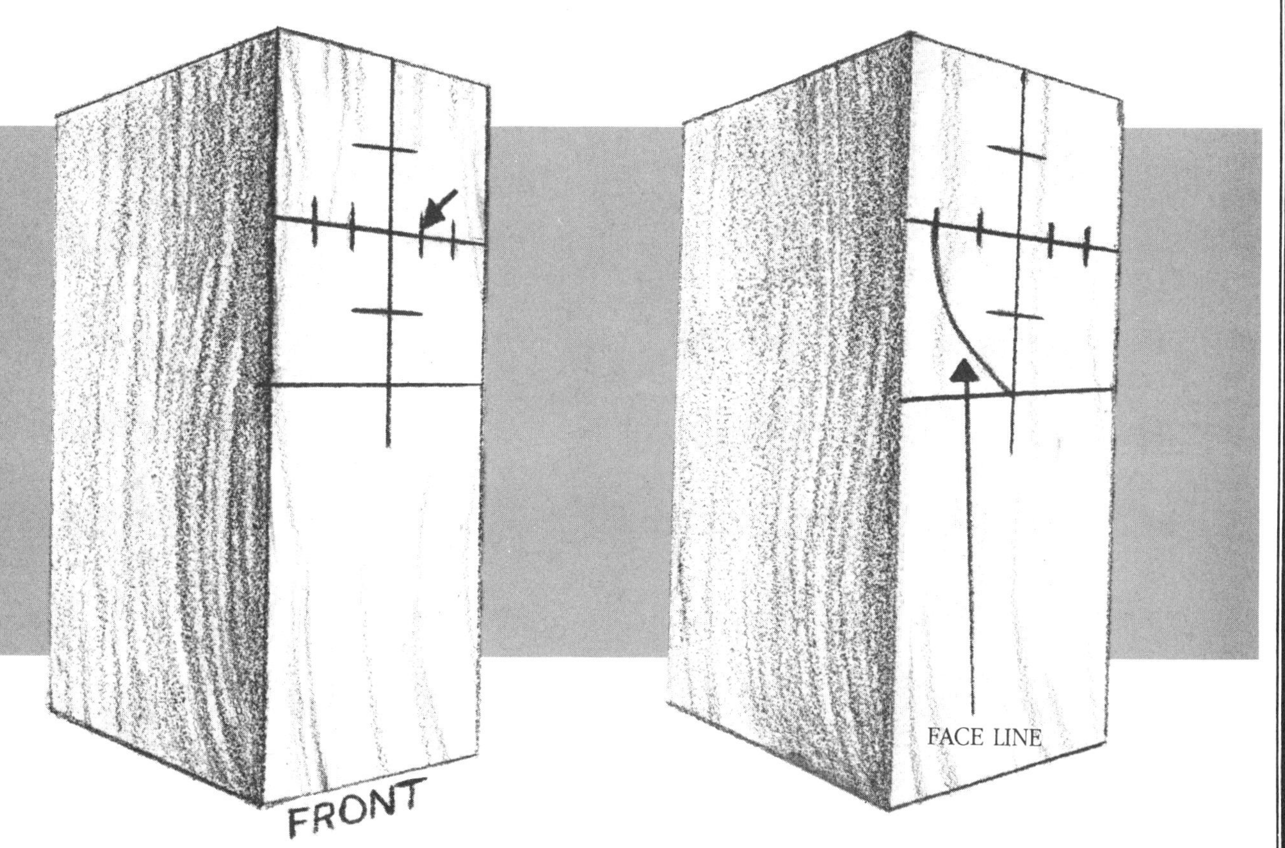

11. Draw a curved face line.

12. The center of the eyes are on the lines nearest the center line. ➤

13. Divide the side of the block into three equal sections. Shape the hairline 2/3" of the way back to the top of the head. ➤

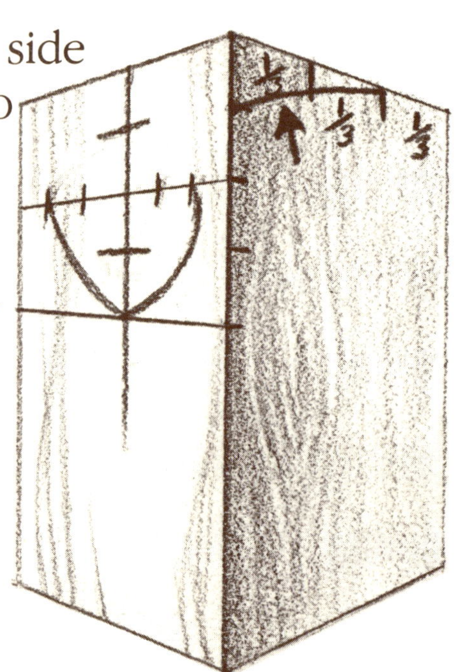

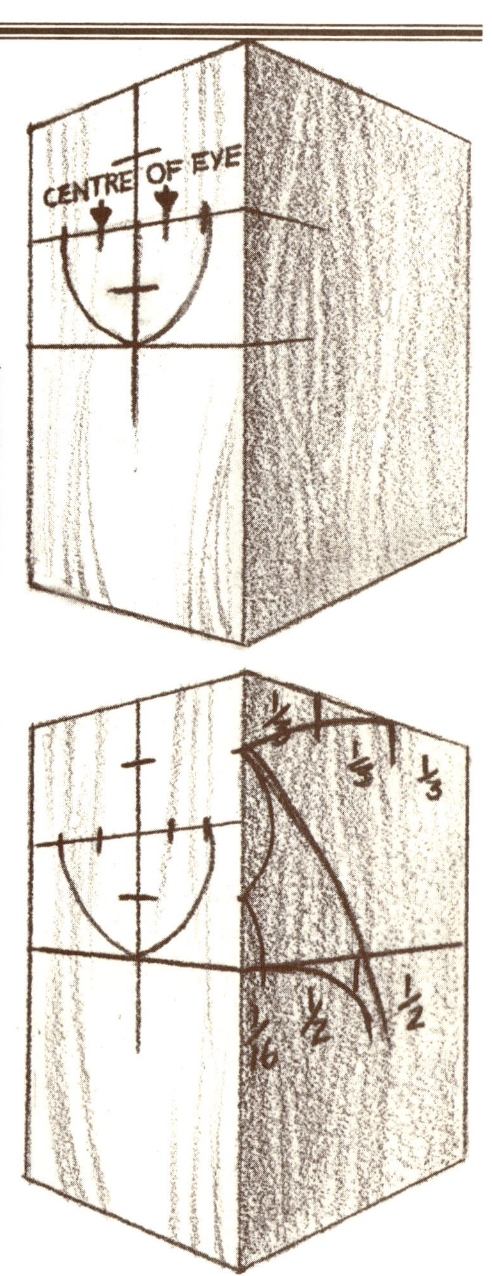

14. Draw an arc beginning ⅛" back from the hairline to the tip of the nose. Depth of this arc should be 1/6 of the way to a center vertical line. Draw a second arc from the tip of the nose to this same depth at the chin line. ➤

SECTION 2

BEGIN CARVING

1. Using a #2 ½ 35-mm shallow gouge, begin carving the top front of the head. Extra pressure and control may be applied by using chest or shoulder as a brace. Complete these cuts using the inside of the gouge.

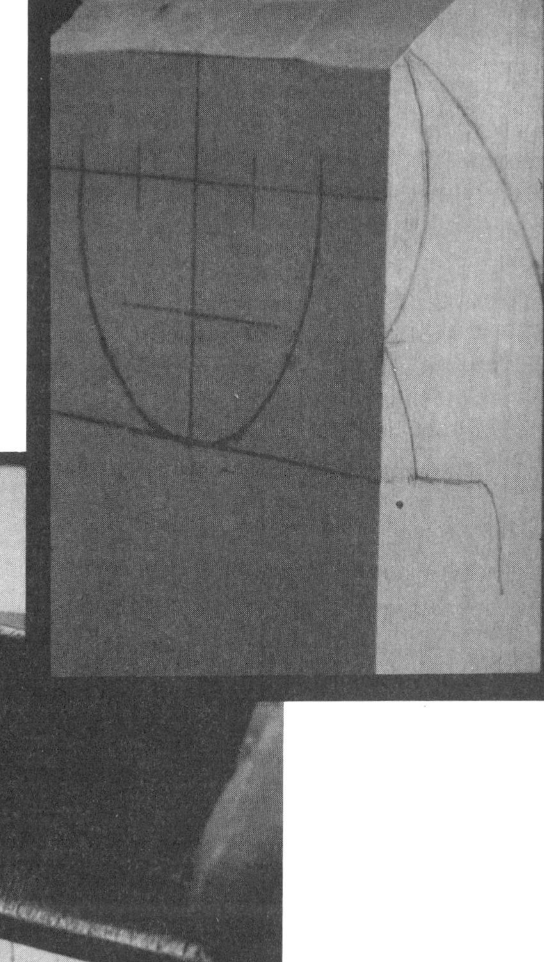

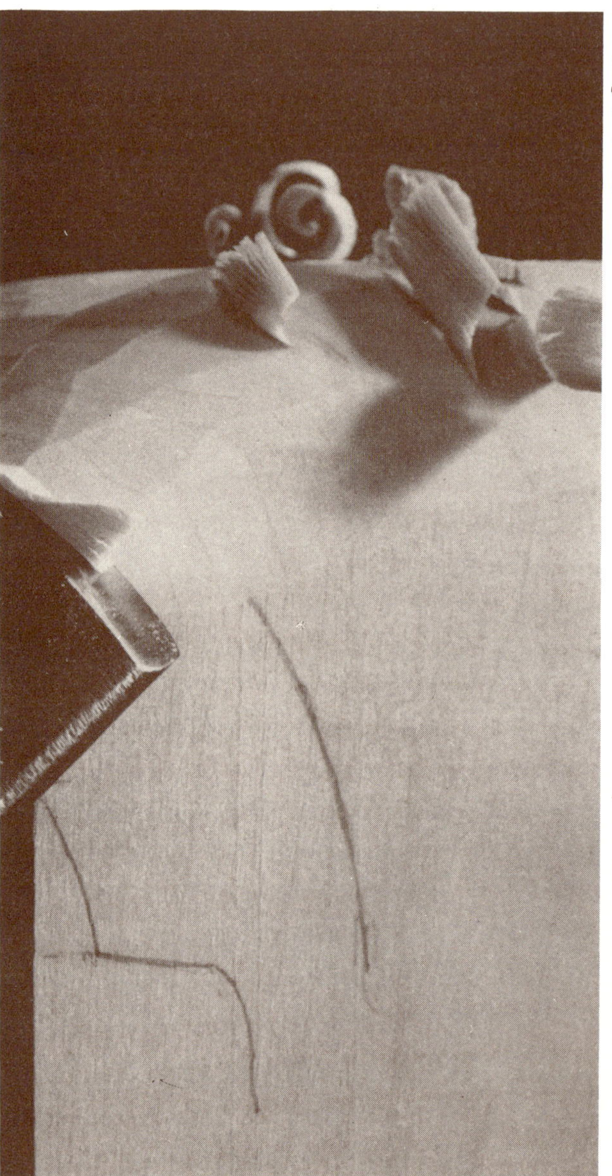

2. Round off the sides of the block from the nose line to the hairline. Repeat on the other side of the block.

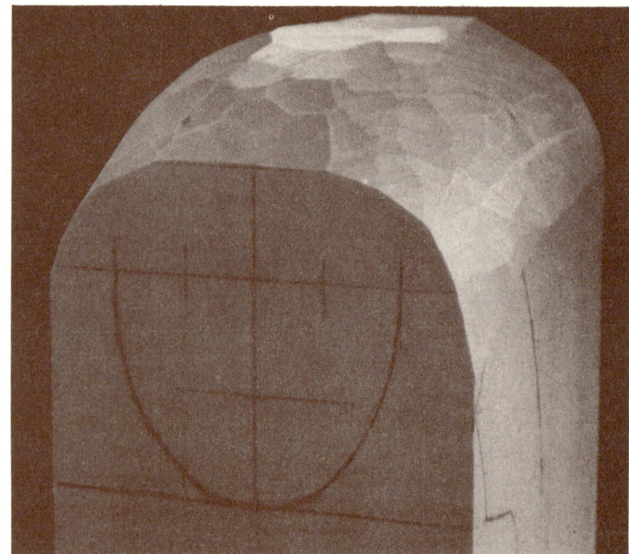

3. Using a #6 18-mm gouge, remove wood at the eye line. Carve a hollow straight across the face.

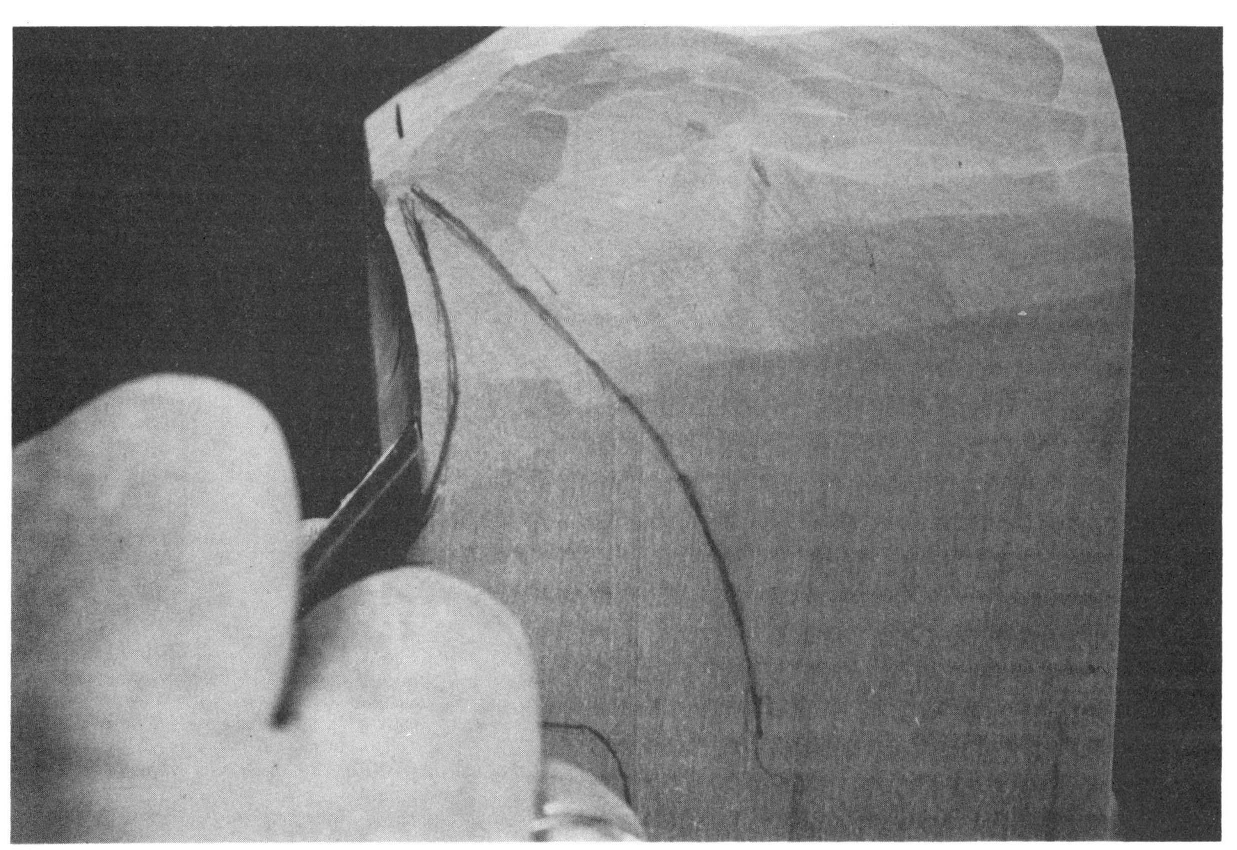

4. With a #6 18-mm gouge, round from vertical center of the eye to side hairline. Care against splitting should be taken when cutting against the grain. Using the same gouge, continue to round off the sides of the face.

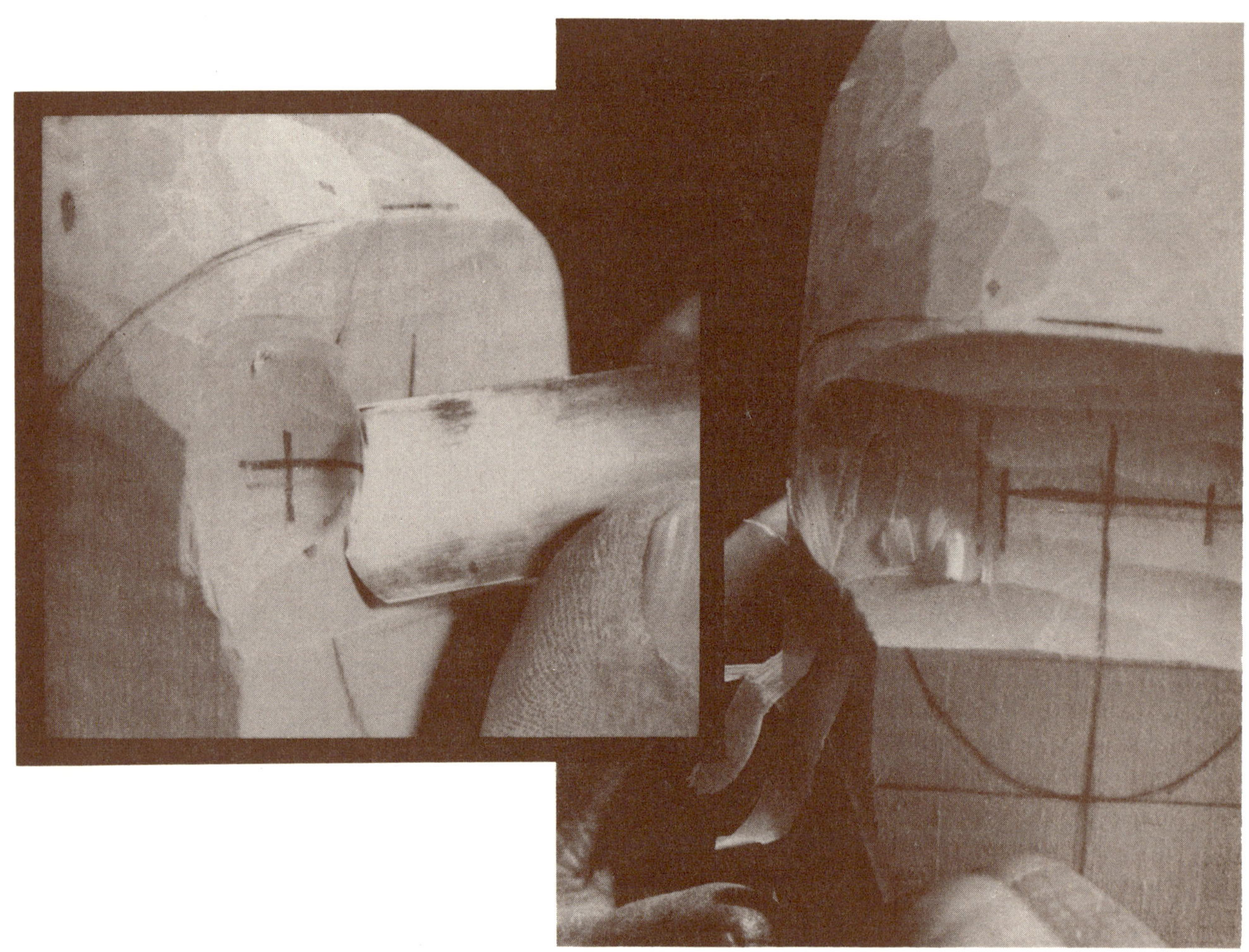

Arrows indicate the best directions for cutting.

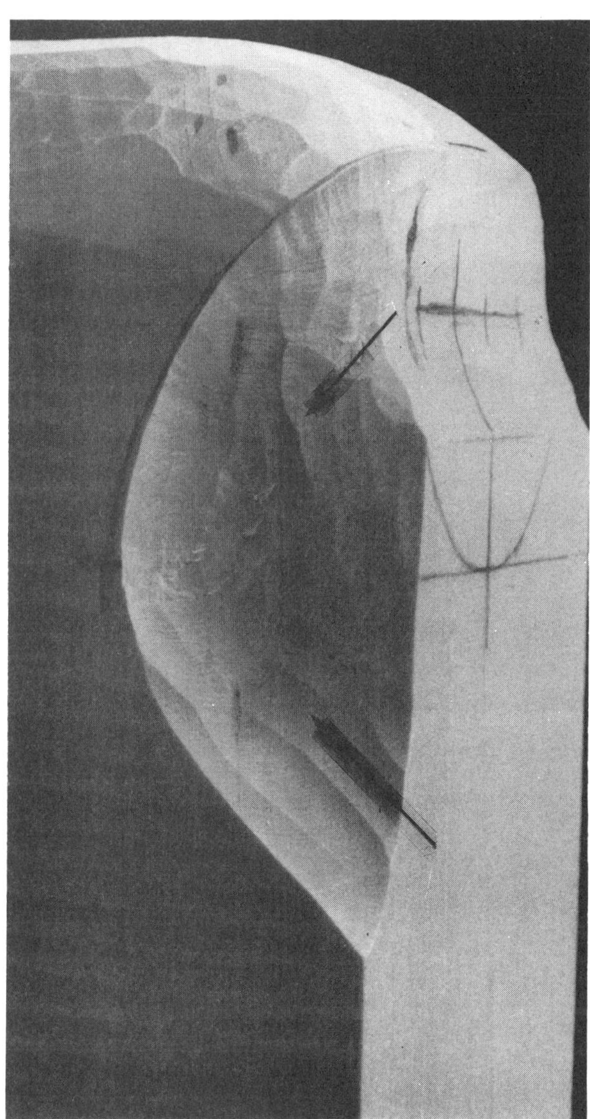

5. Repeat the process for the other side of the face.

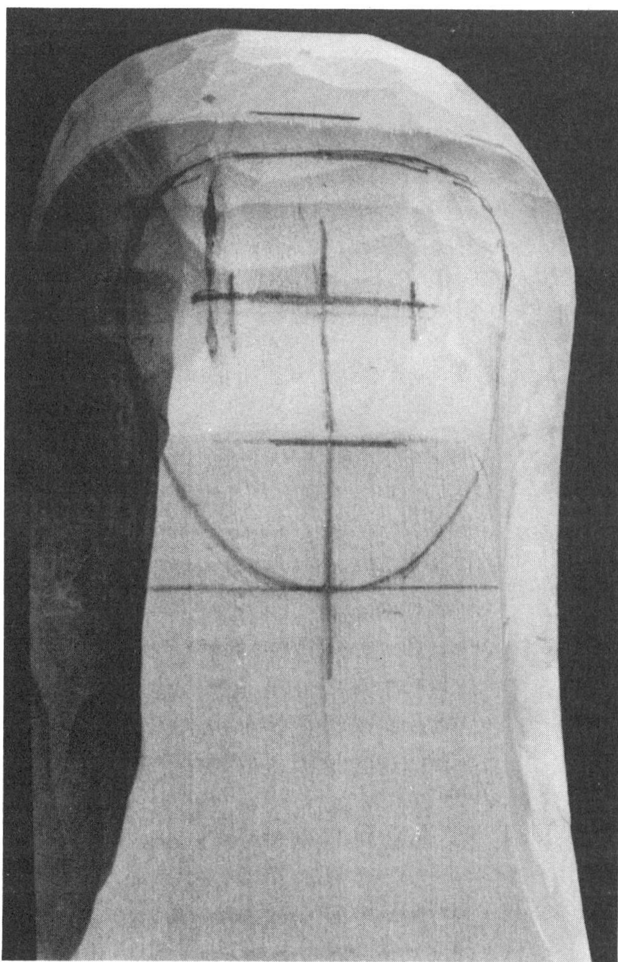

HINT: Control your cuts by placing your second hand on the carving.

6. Redraw the outline of the face using the original lines.

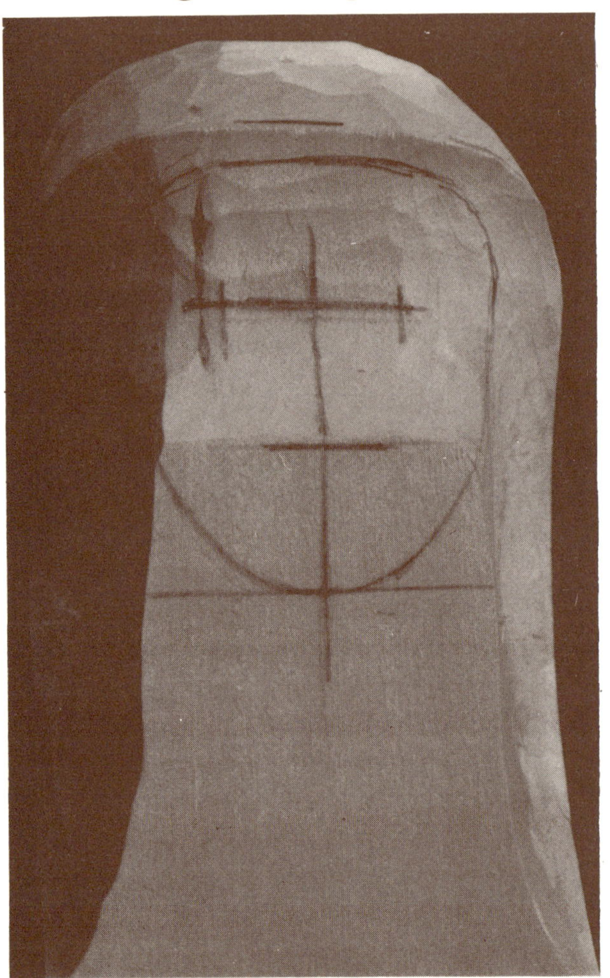

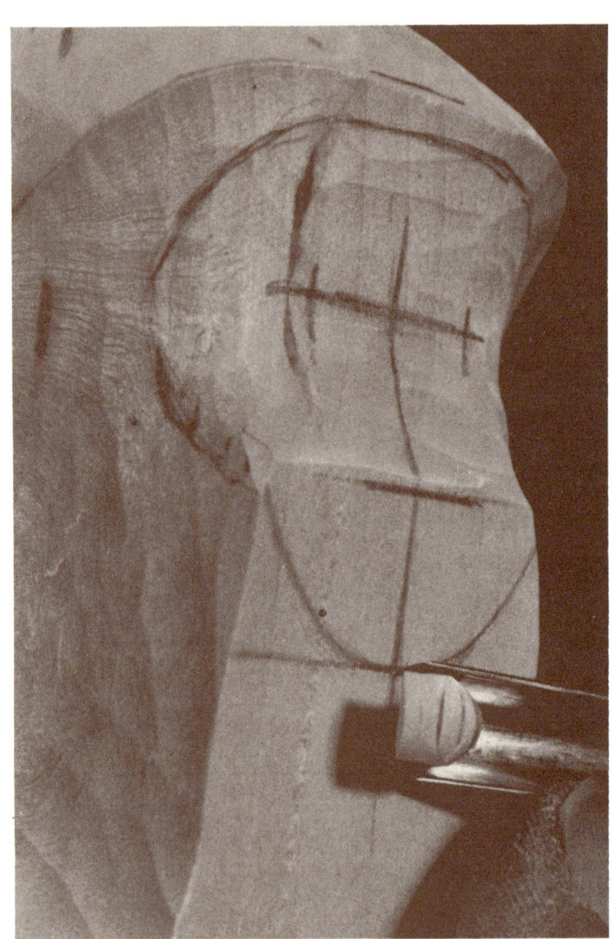

7. Using a #11 10-mm gouge, make a cross cut below the chin line about 1" deep.

More than one cut will be required to obtain the one-inch depth.

8. Using a #2 ½ 35-mm gouge, round off the sides of the face from the eye line to chin.

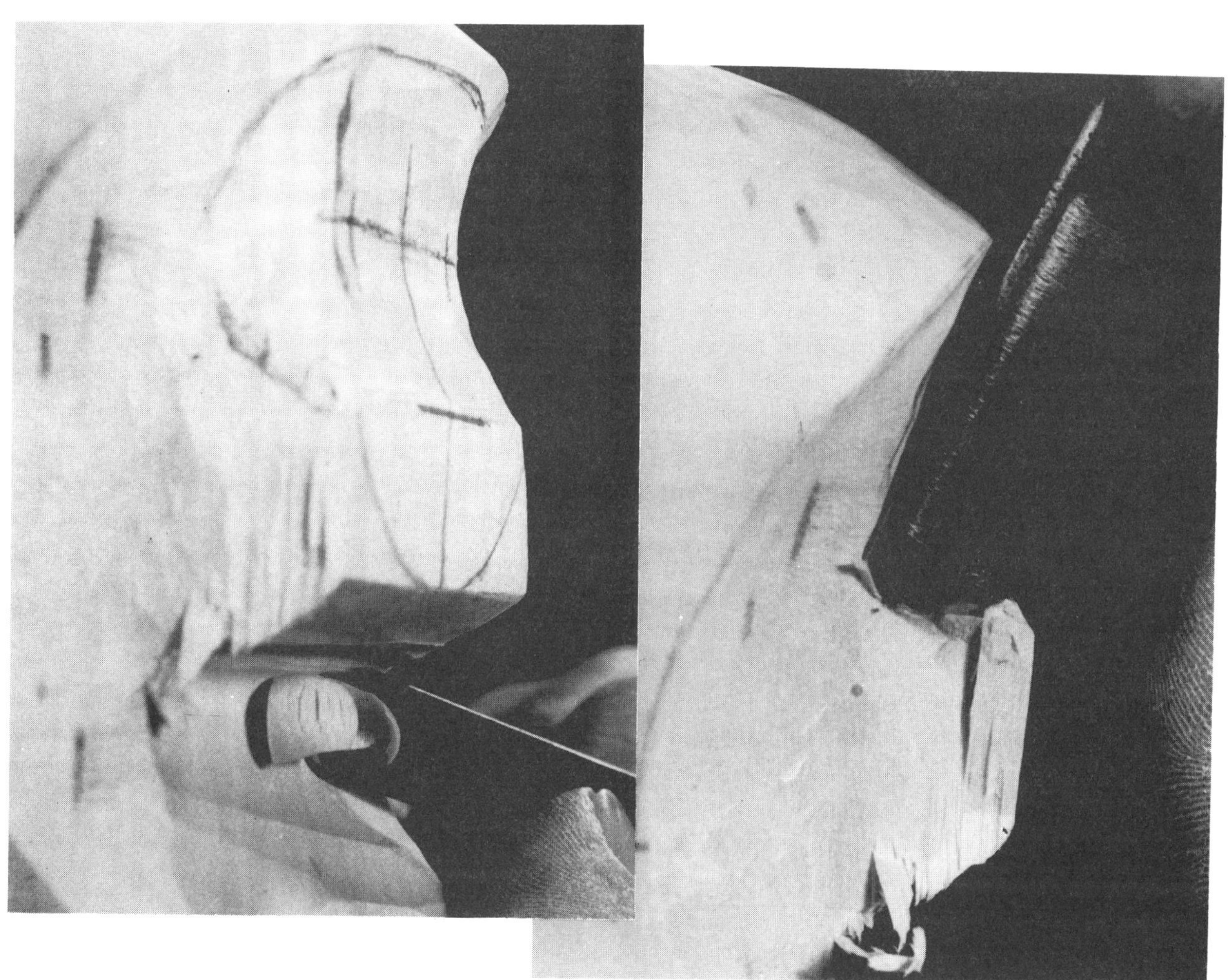

Clean up your cuts with a #11 10-mm gouge.

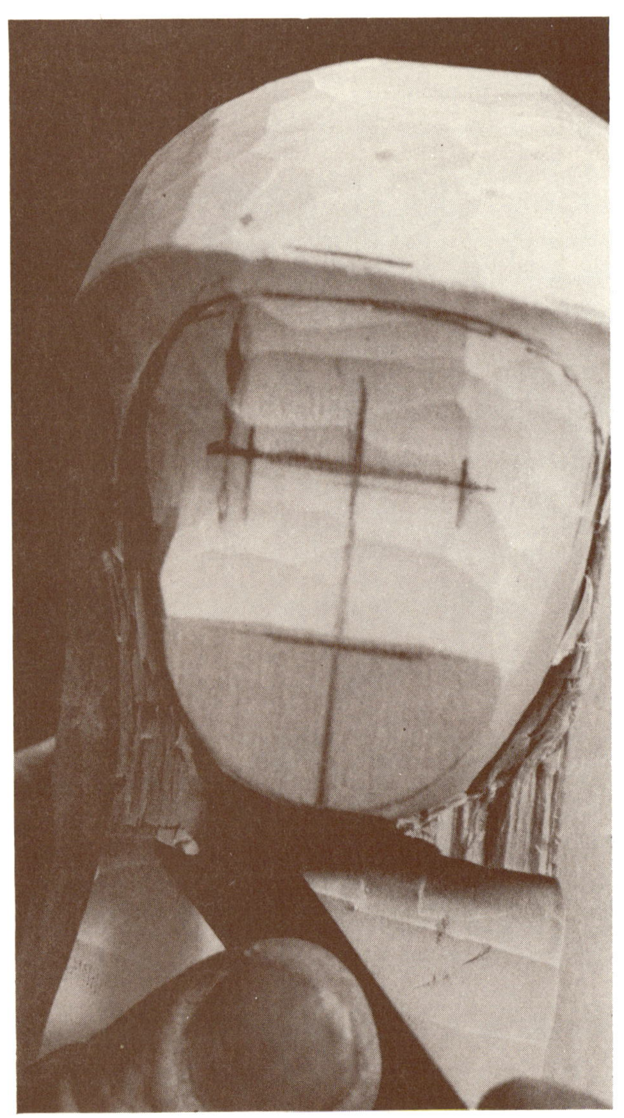

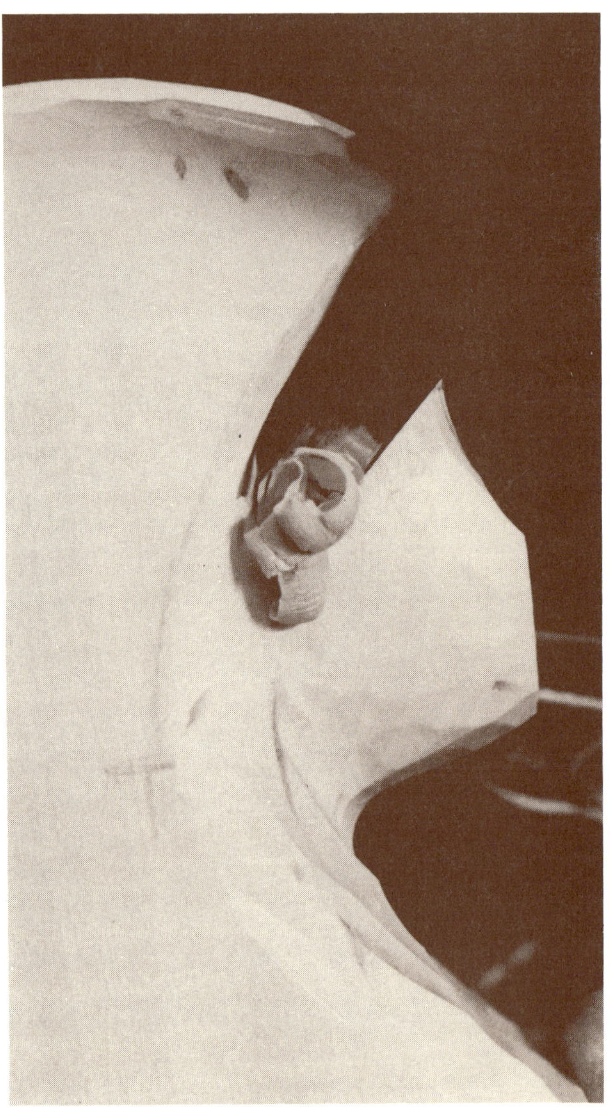

9. Using the same gouge, define the hair line...

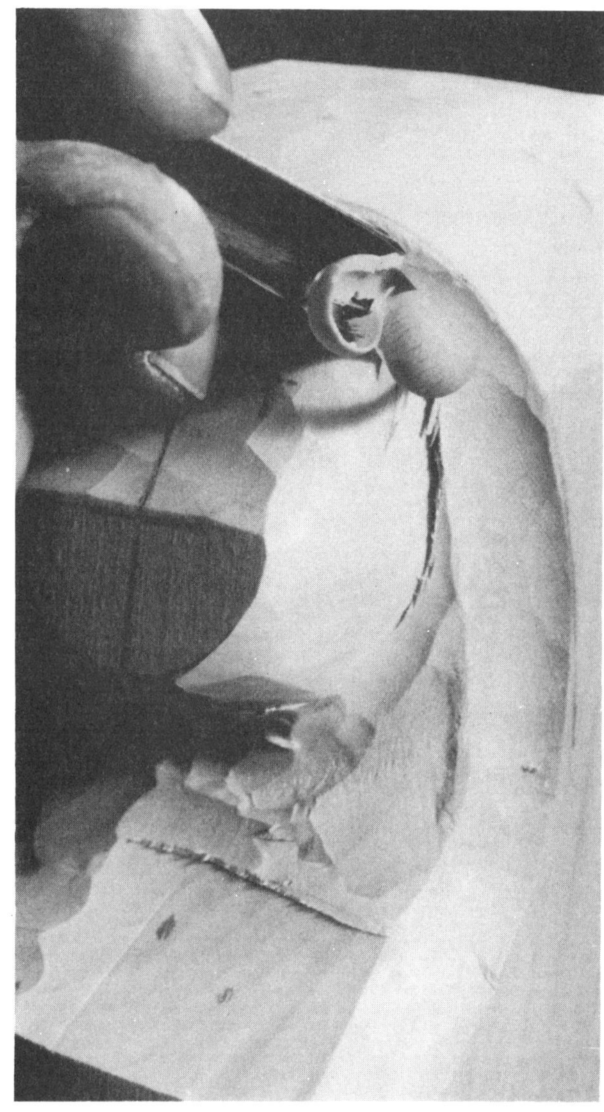

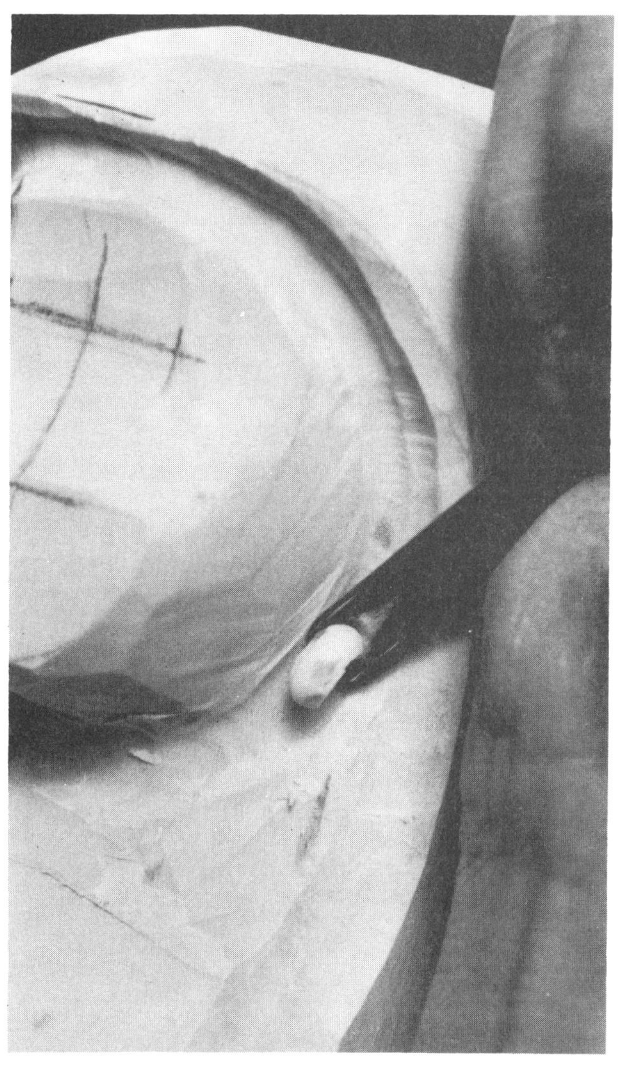

...and the face line.

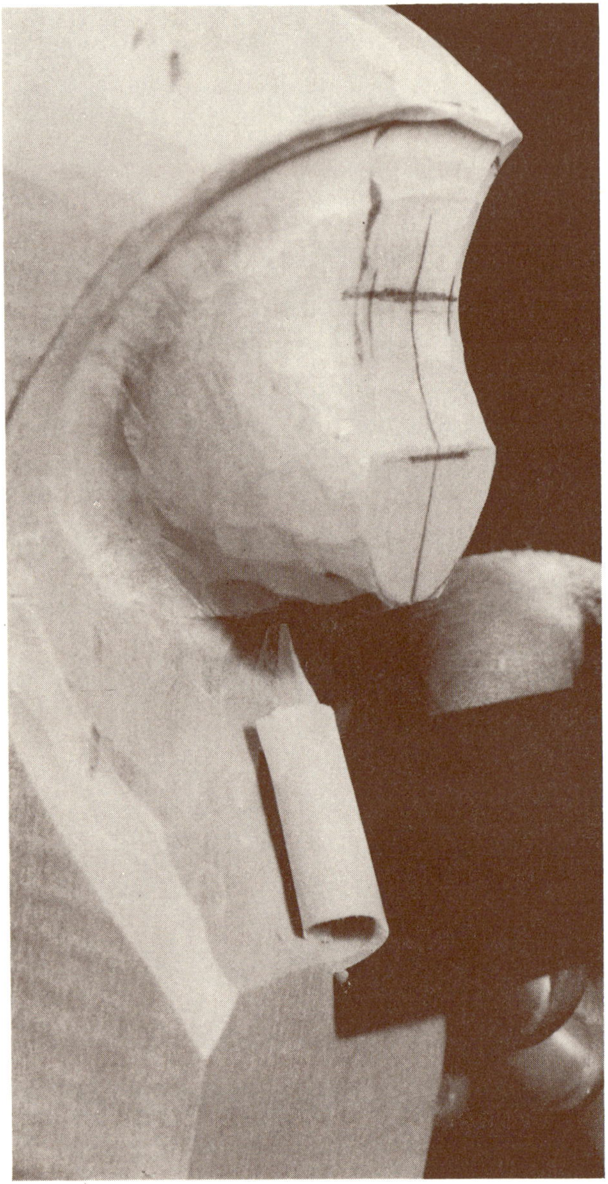

10. With your #2 ½ 35-mm shallow gouge, remove a little excess wood from the neck area.

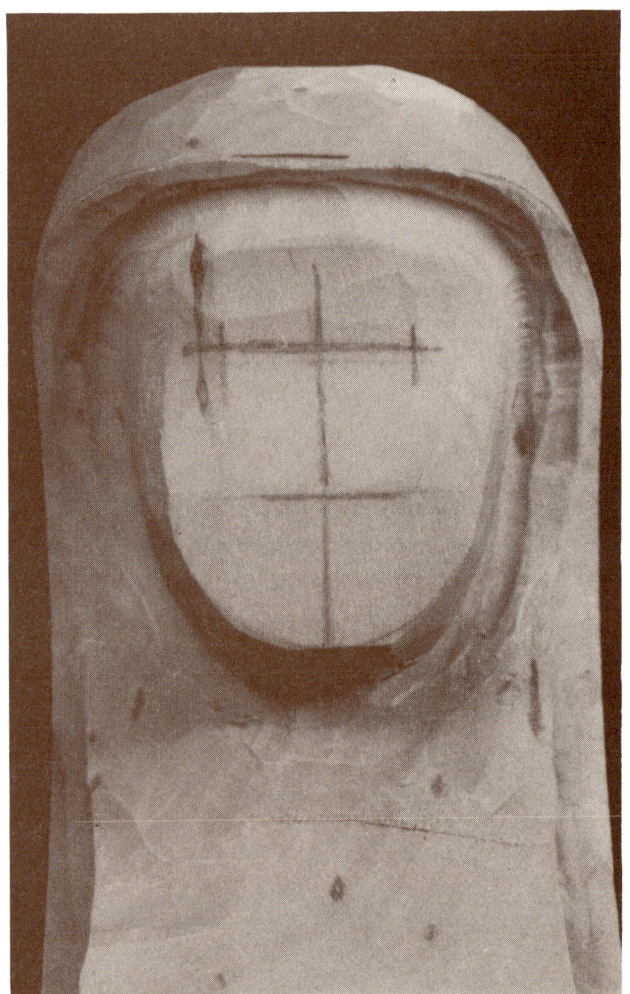

11. Continue defining the face and hairline, checking for symmetry.

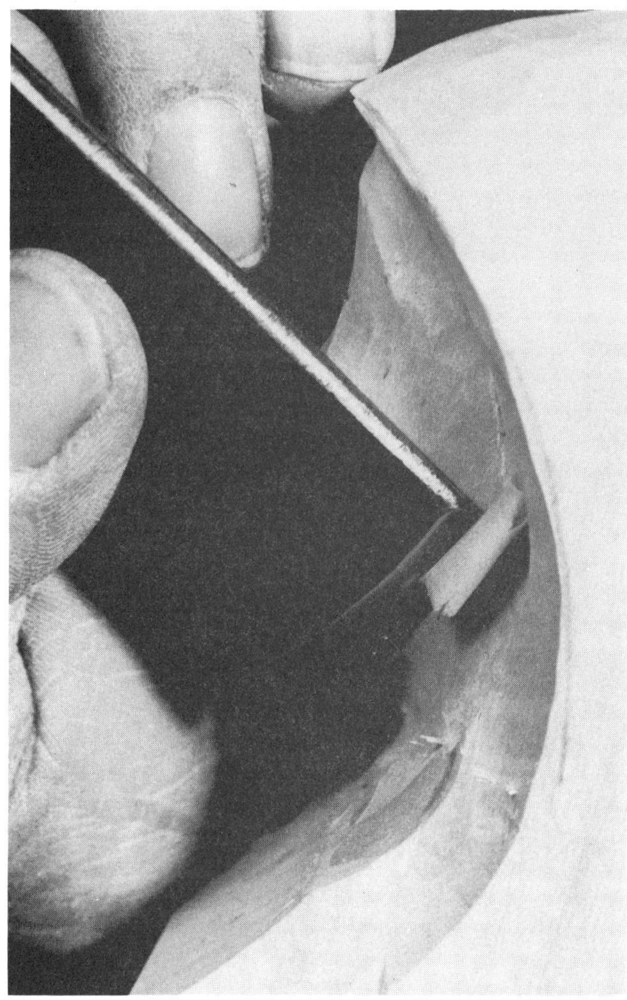

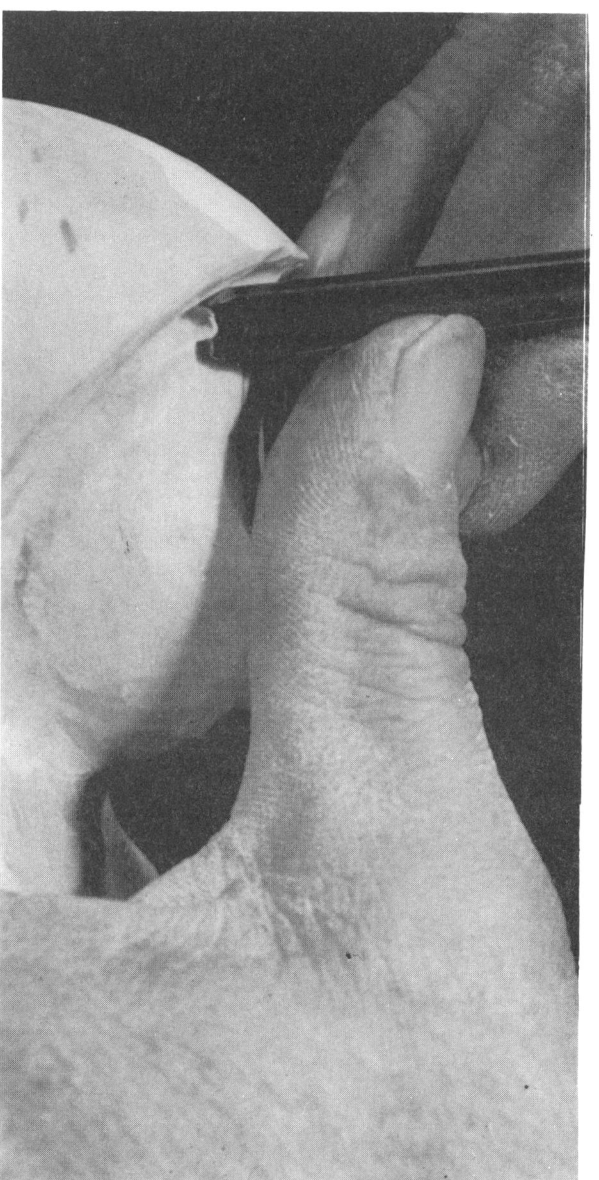

12. Use a #11 6-mm gouge to get closer definiton.

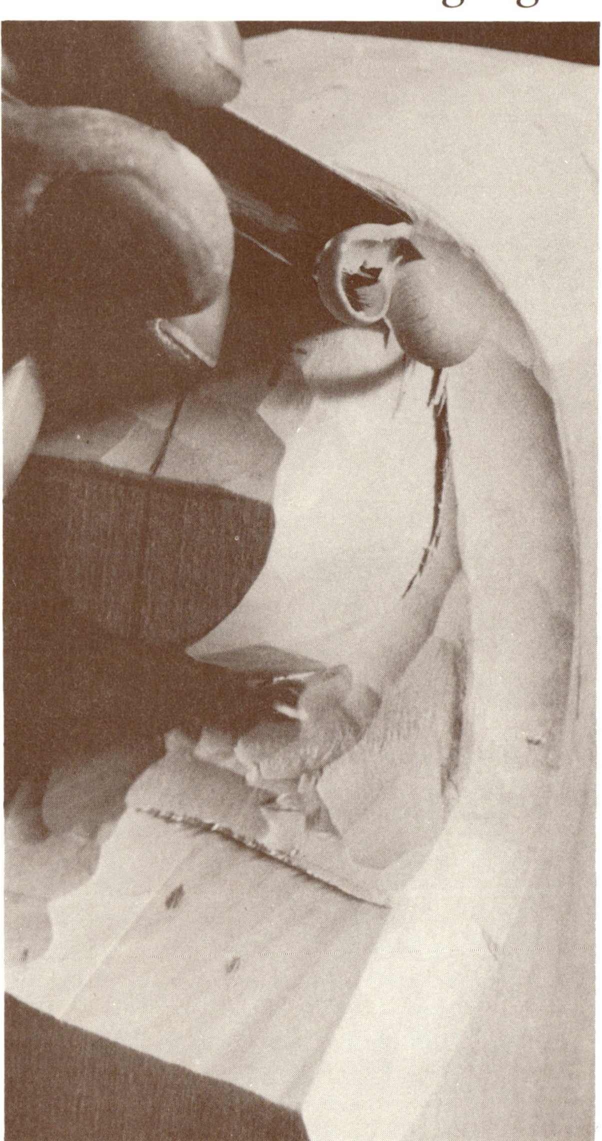

13. Assuming that the hairline occupies a 1/6 section on each side, continue to outline with your #11 6-mm gouge. ▼

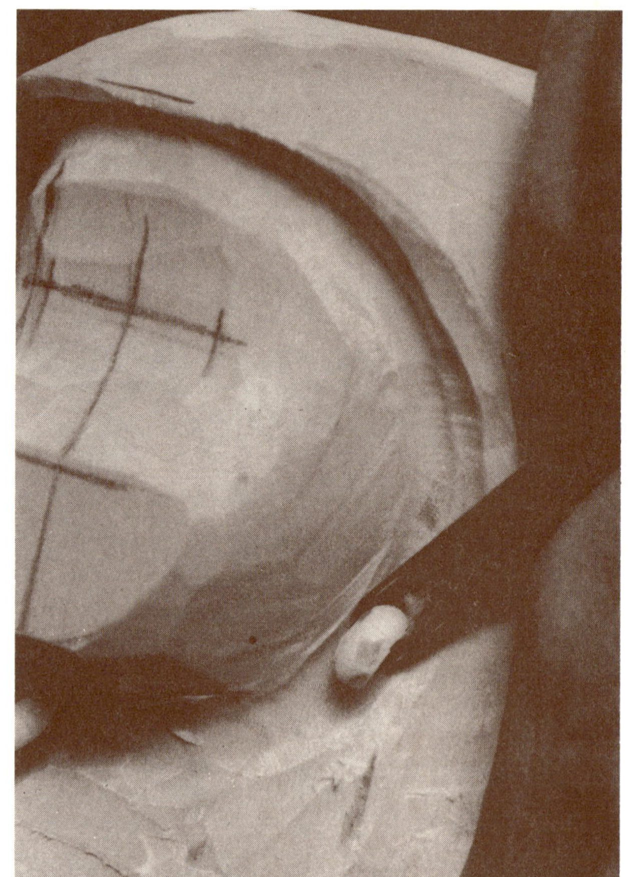

14. Using the same gouge, cut a part for the hair ⅛" deep in front, tapering to 1/16" toward the back of the head.

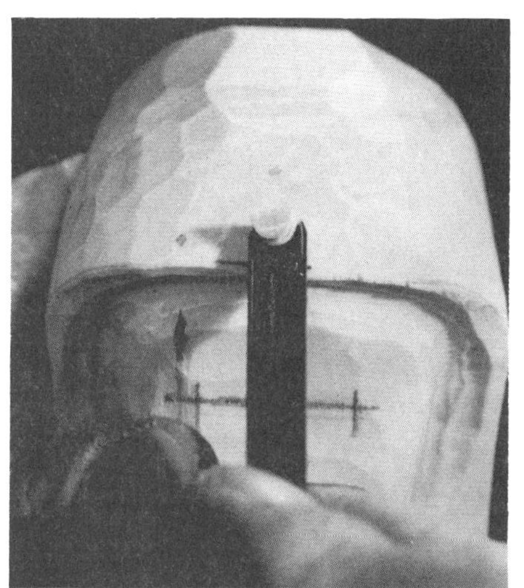

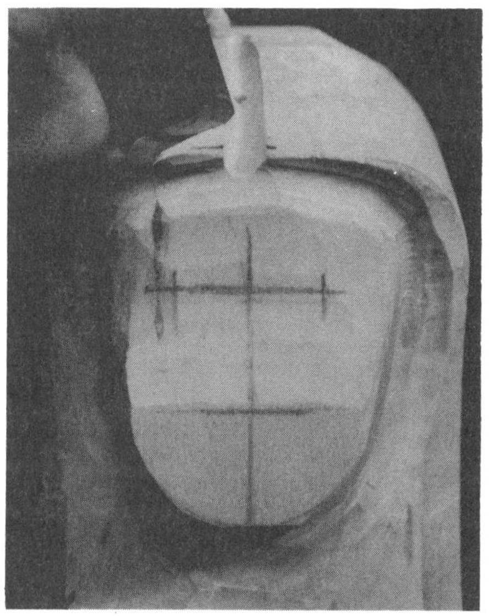

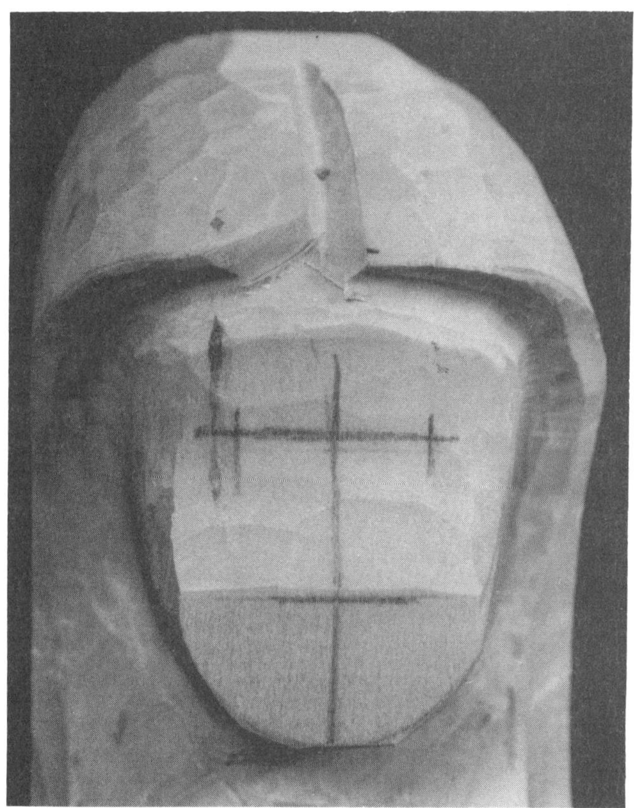

15. A #4 18-mm gouge is used to remove sharp edges and establish a flowing hair line. The forehead may be smoothed with a skew.

16. Mark the section below the nose to the chin as shown. ▼

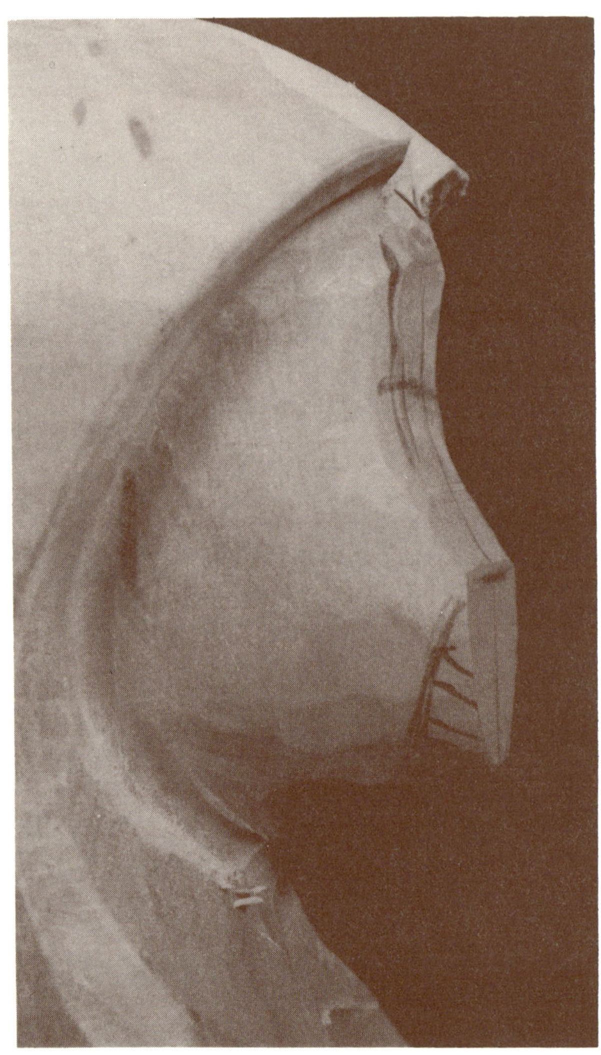

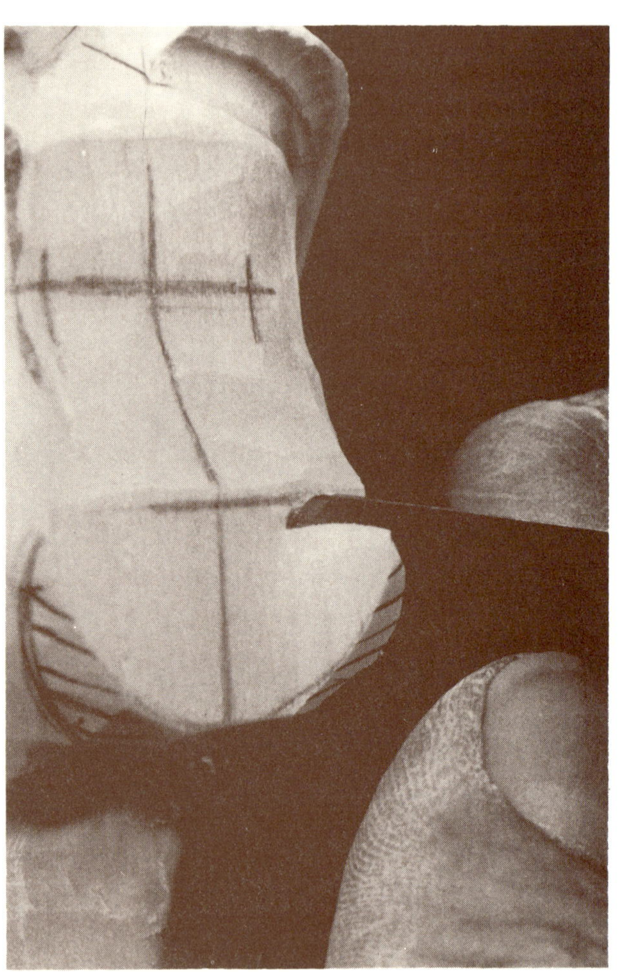

17. With a #6 18-mm gouge, remove this section in a straight cut across. ▲

SECTION 3

CARVING THE EYES

1. An eye-spacing cut must be made at about 60 degrees to establish the taper for the side of the nose and the depth of the eye. This crescent-shaped chip of wood should be removed by lifting the chisel handle with a slight upward pressure.

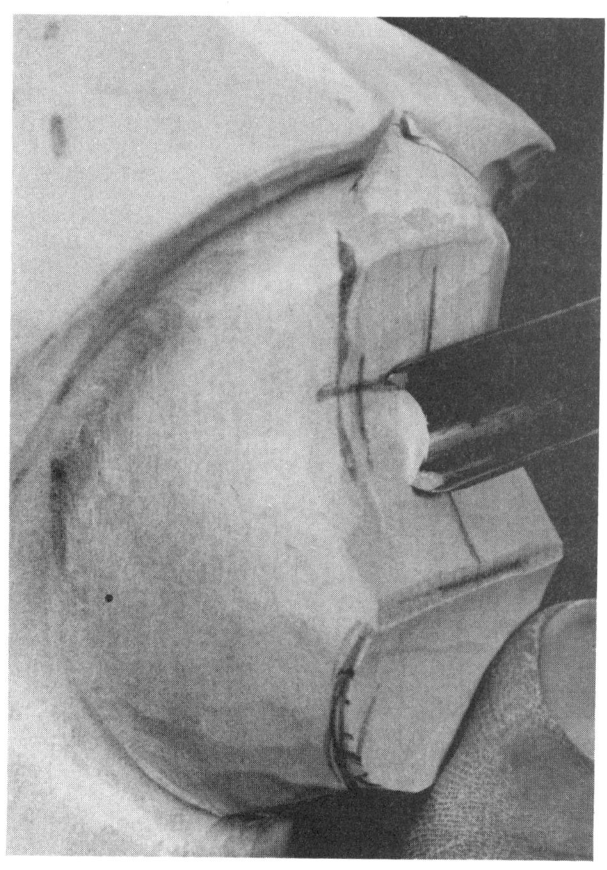

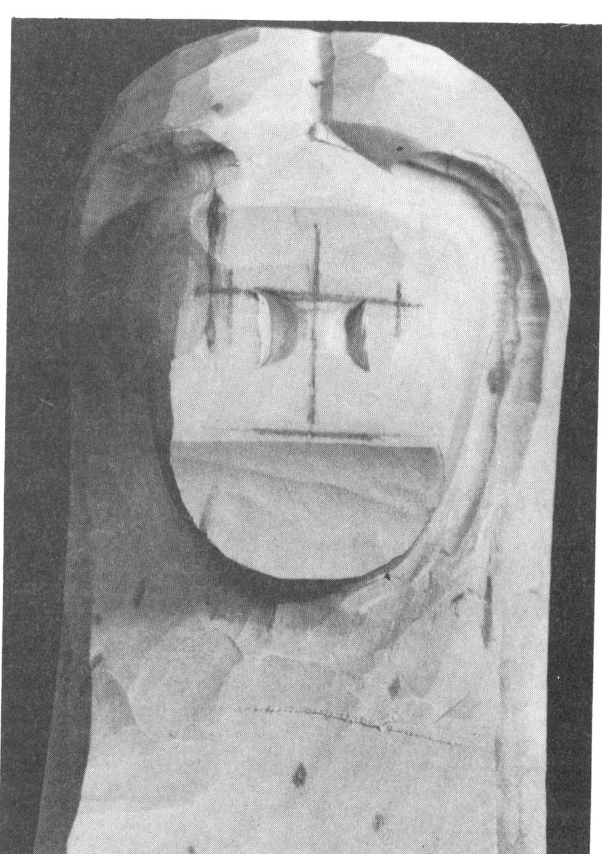

2. Use a #9 10-mm gouge to make an upward cut from below the nose, defining the side of the nose and ending at the crescent cut of the eye.

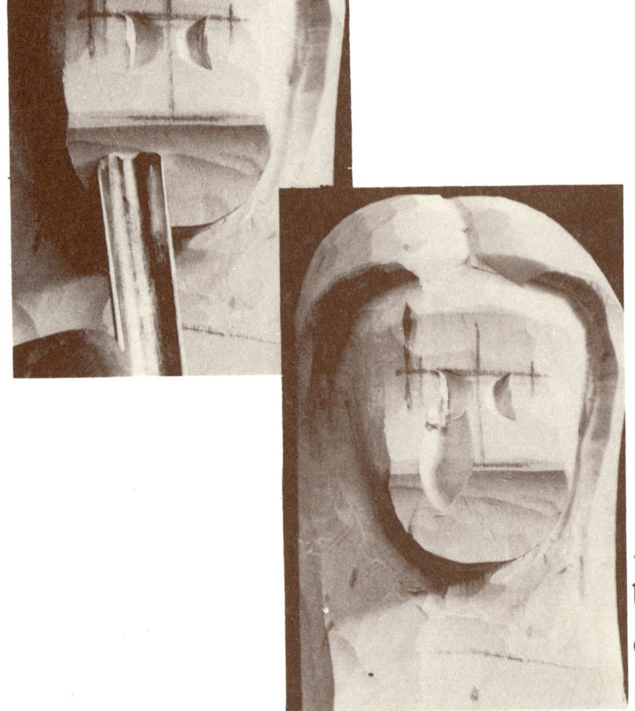

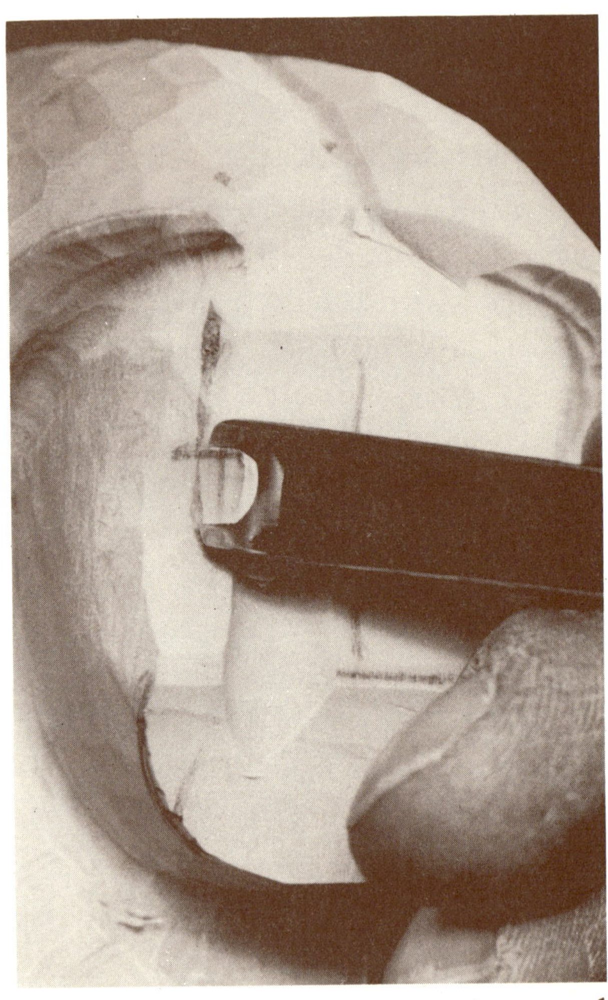

3. A #9 10-mm gouge is used to make a third cut which is a cross cut to shape the top of the eye and eyelid.

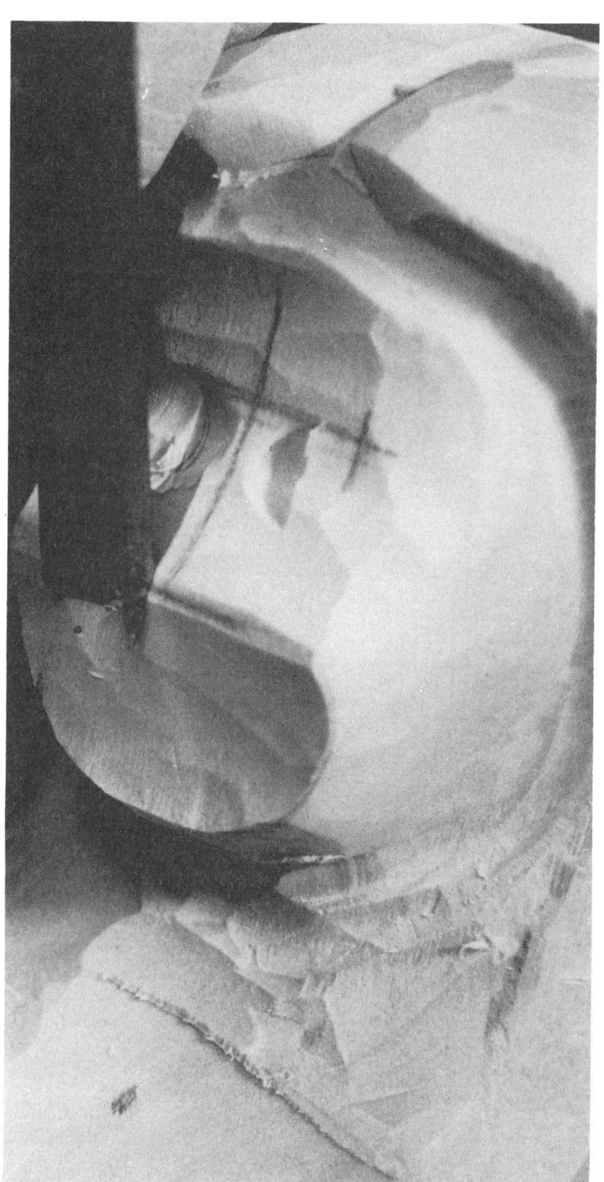

4. Using a #9 10-mm gouge, extend the cut at the side of the nose down toward the outside and bottom of the chin. This will create a better perspective to continue work on the eye.

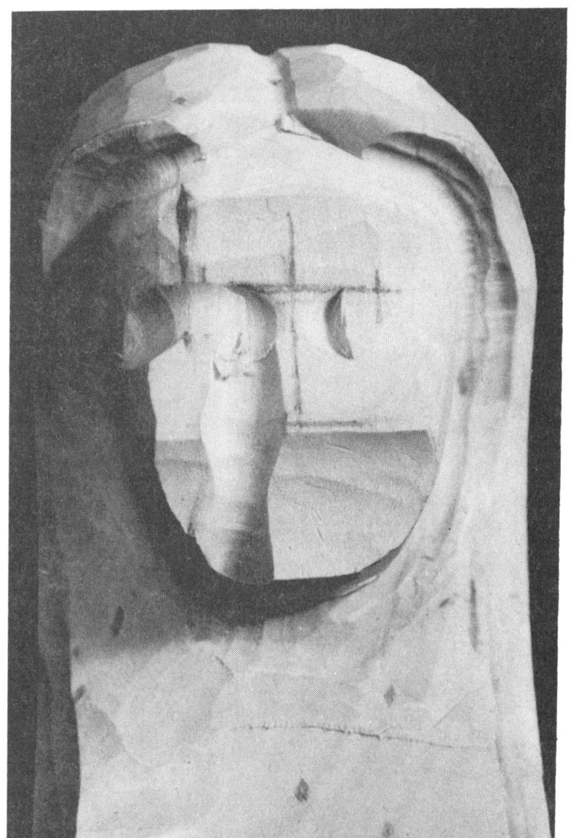

5. Using the bottom of the third eye cut as a guide, place your #9 10-mm gouge down 3/16" from the top edge and make a cross cut to the same depth as the vertical nose cut. You now have a rough eyelid location. This will be raised on later cuts.

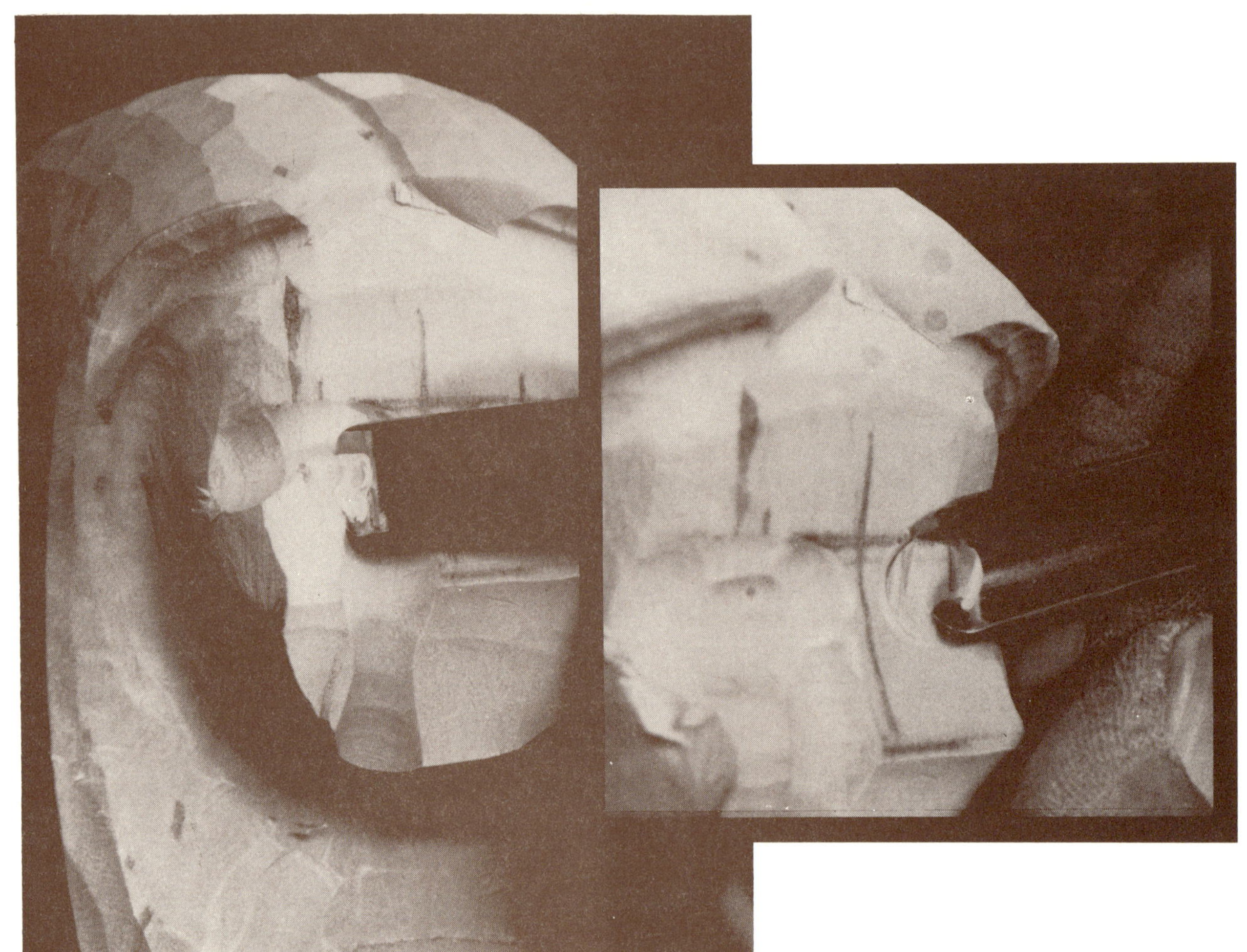

Repeat this procedure on the other eye.

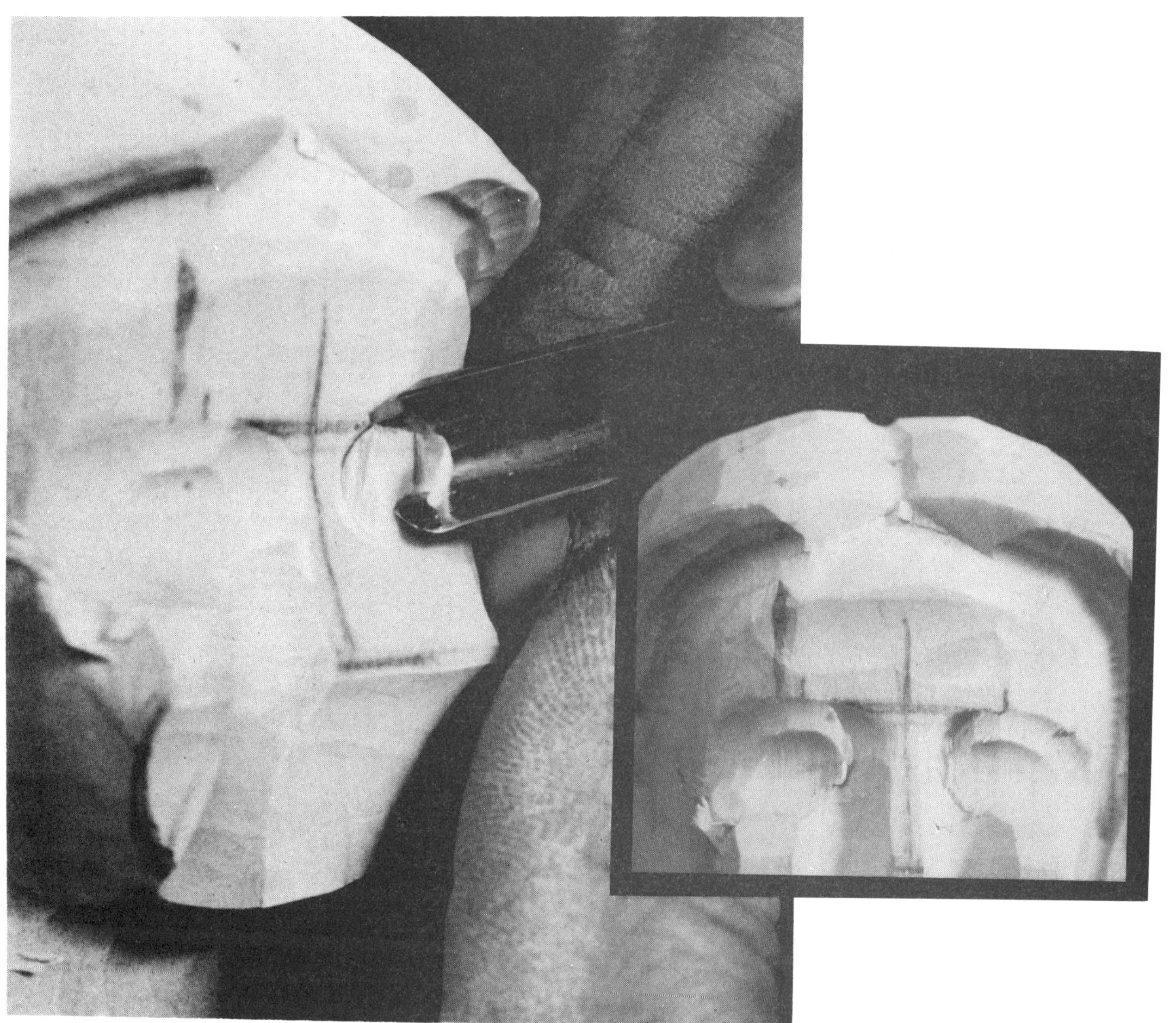

SECTION 4

CARVING THE NOSE

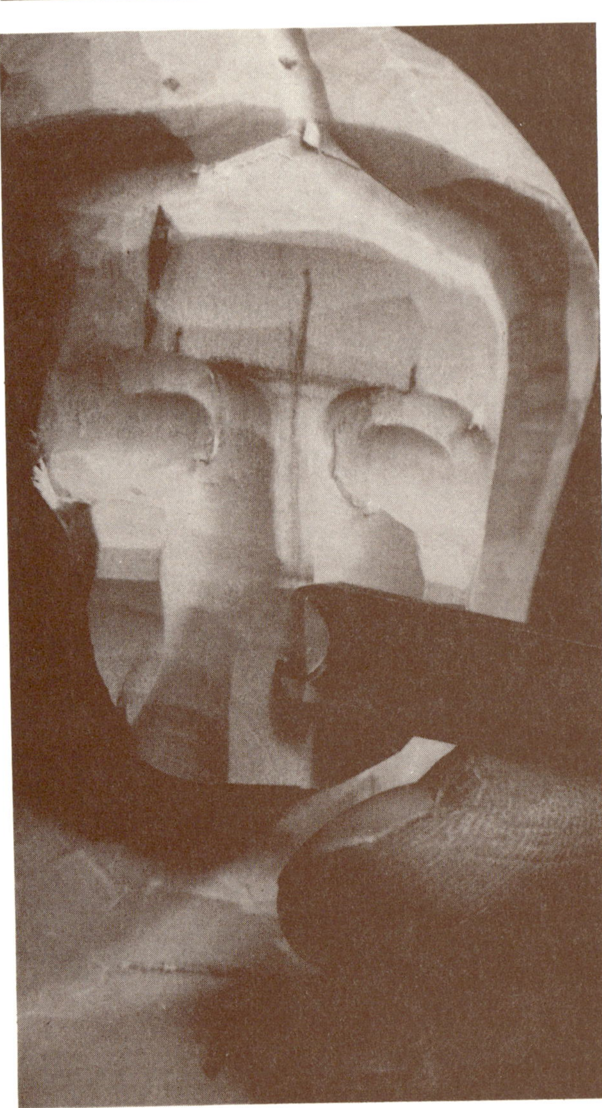

1. Using a #9 10-mm gouge, make a short ⅛"-deep cut below the nose, stopping before it reaches the vertical cut.

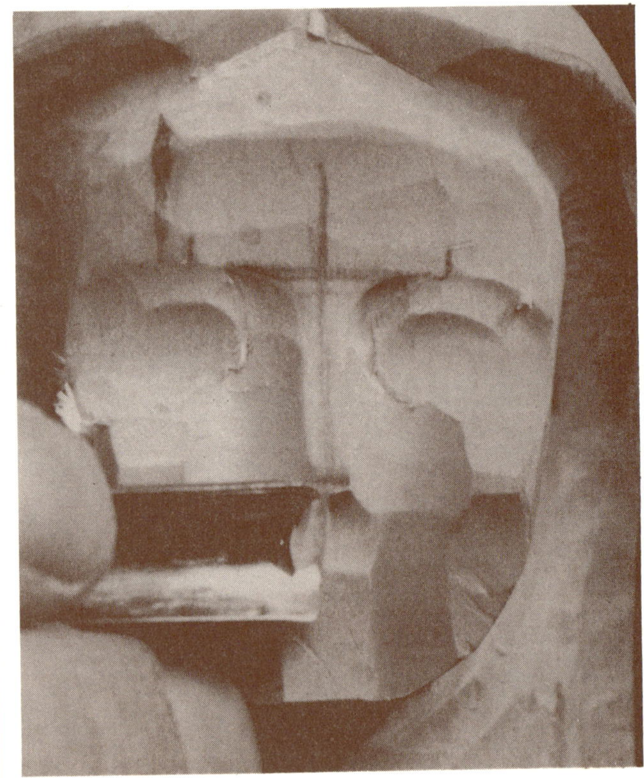

Continue the cut from the other side.

2. Continuing with a #9 10-mm gouge, using the ridge from the previous cut as a center line, make the next cut ¼" wide.

3. Using the bottom of the previous cut again as the center line, repeat the cut to form the lower lip and the chin. ➤

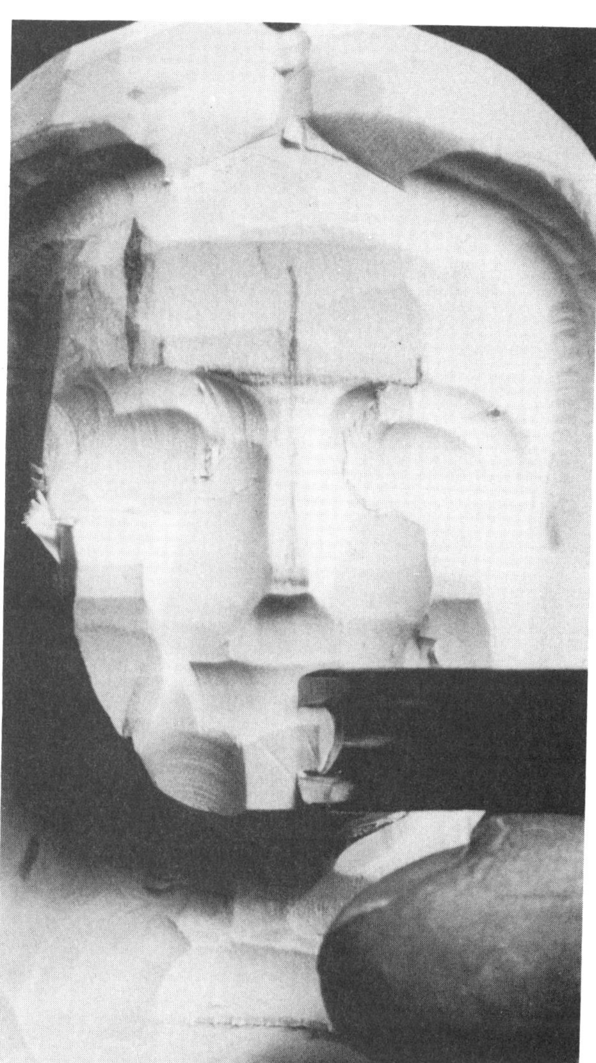

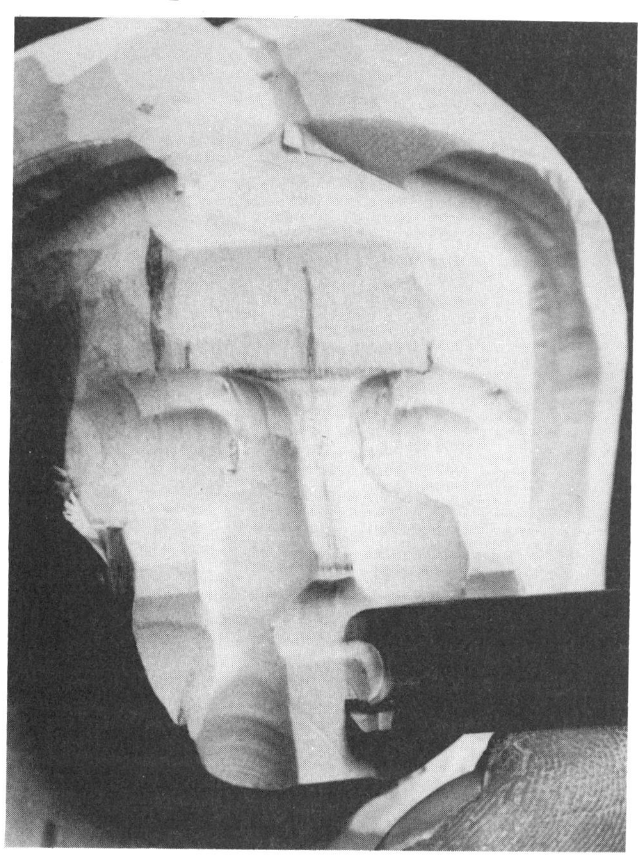

4. To round off the cheek, use a #2 ½ 18-mm gouge to remove excess wood from the cheek, starting at the mouth line and move up toward the eye with a curved motion. ➤

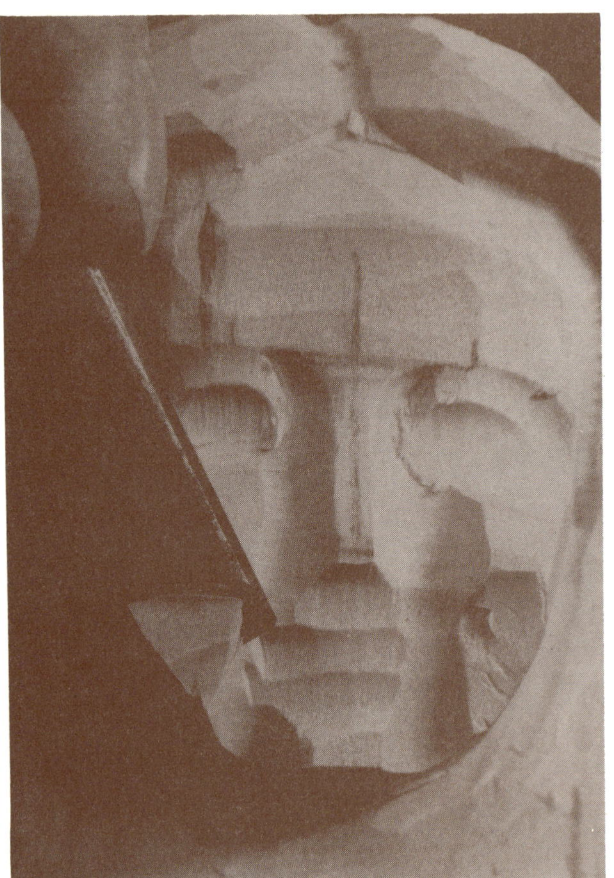

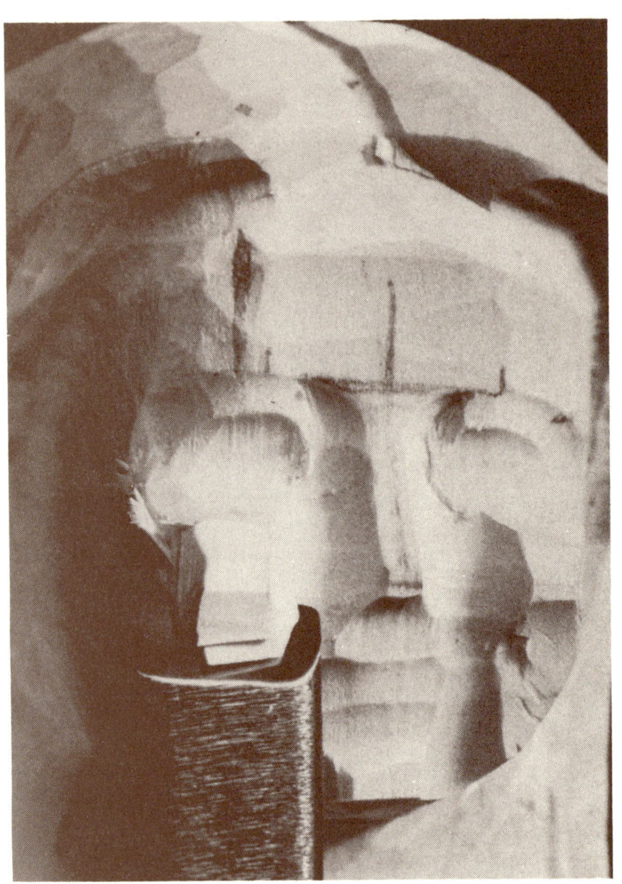

5. With the same shallow gouge, starting at the nose level, remove excess wood from the cheek with a down-and-back motion, to cause the mouth and chin to protrude. ◄

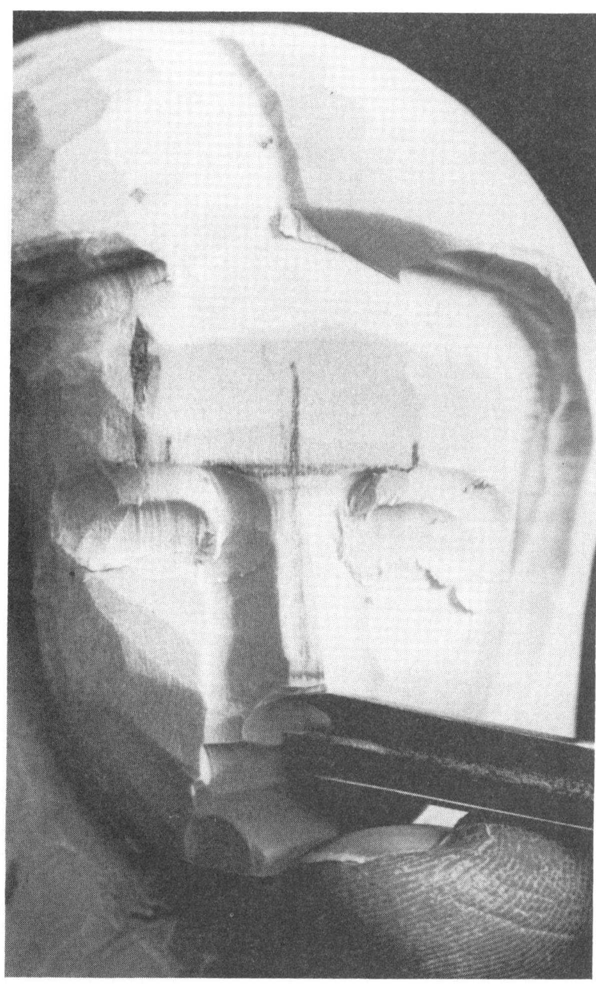

6. With a #11 6-mm gouge, trim more wood from the bottom of the nose, approximately 1/16". ▲

7. Taper both nostrils slightly 1/16" down toward the center of the nose. ▼

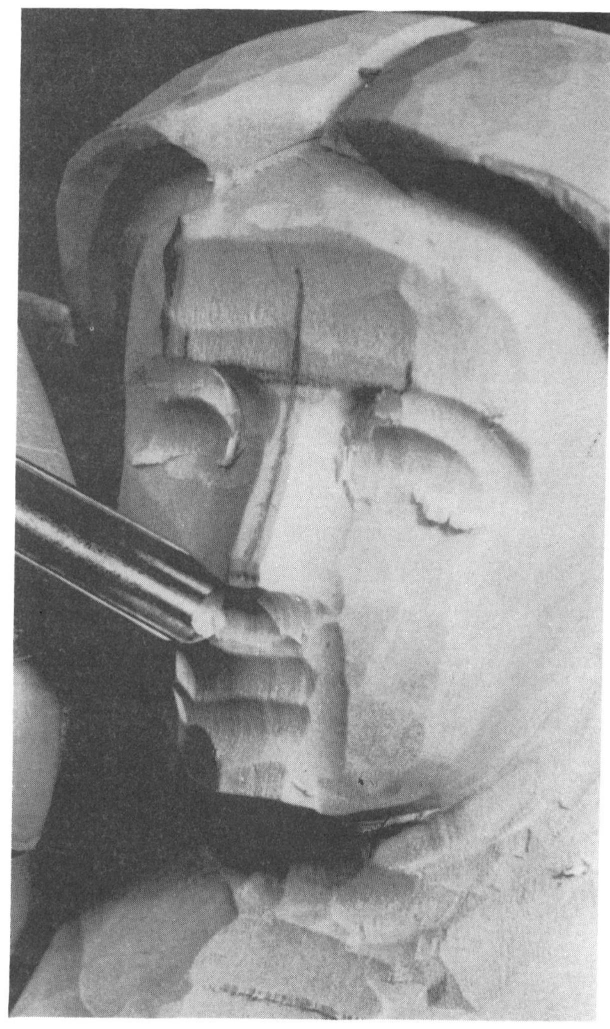

8. Slightly flatten the tip of the nose using a #2 ½ 18-mm shallow gouge.▼

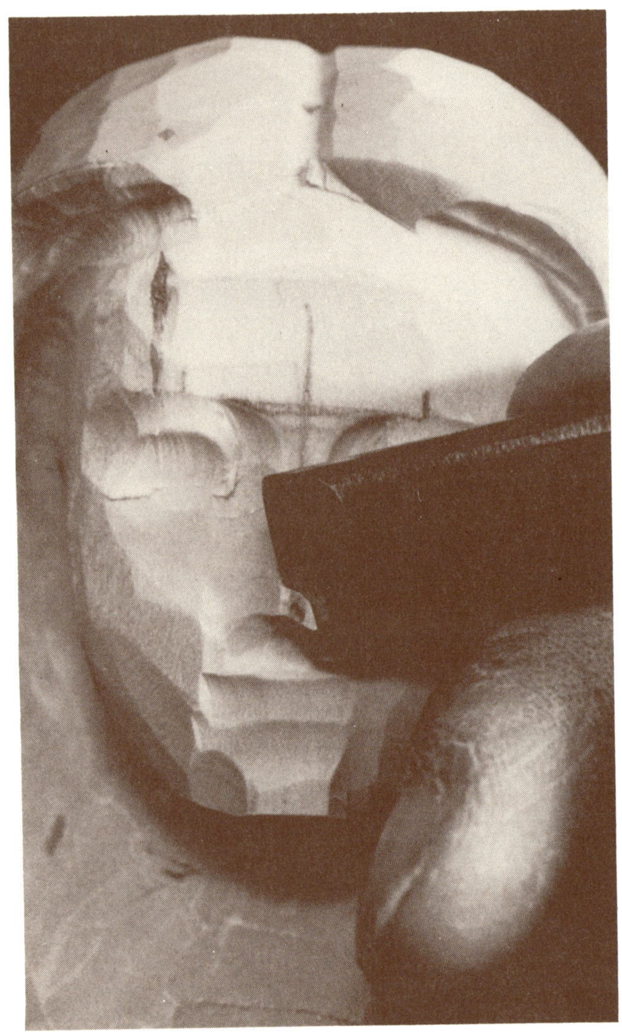

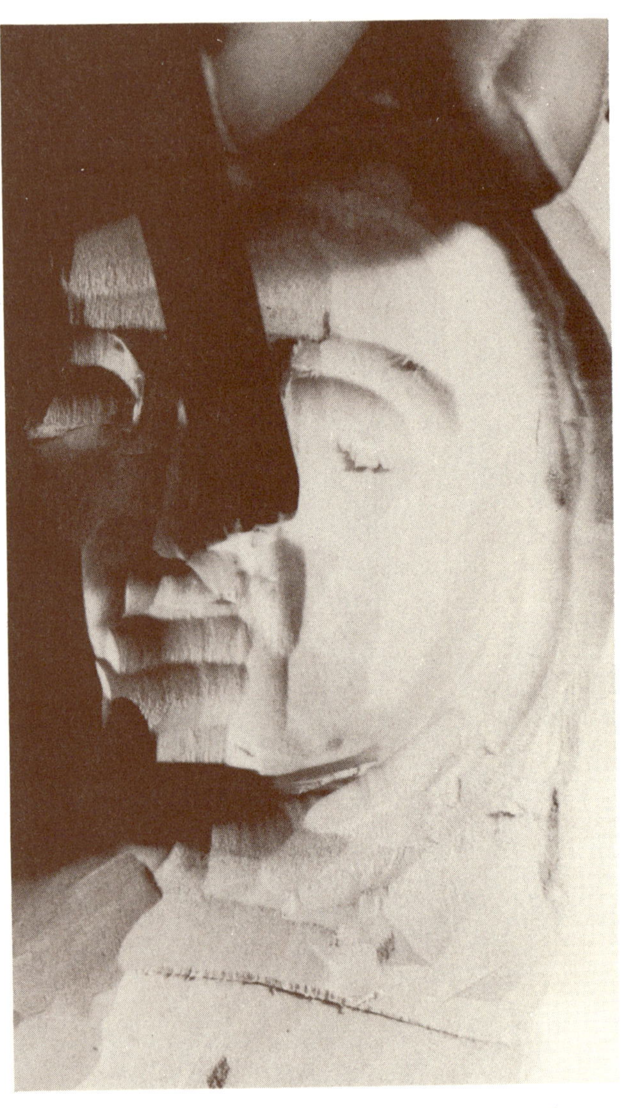

9. Outline the nostrils with a #11 6-mm gouge.▲

Repeat the process on the other side of the nose.

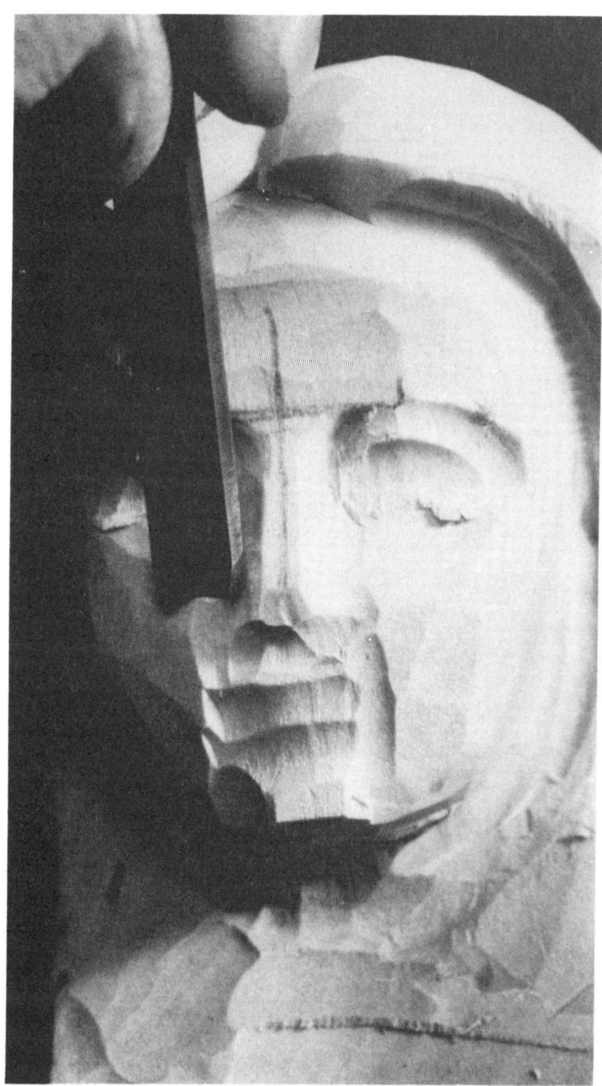

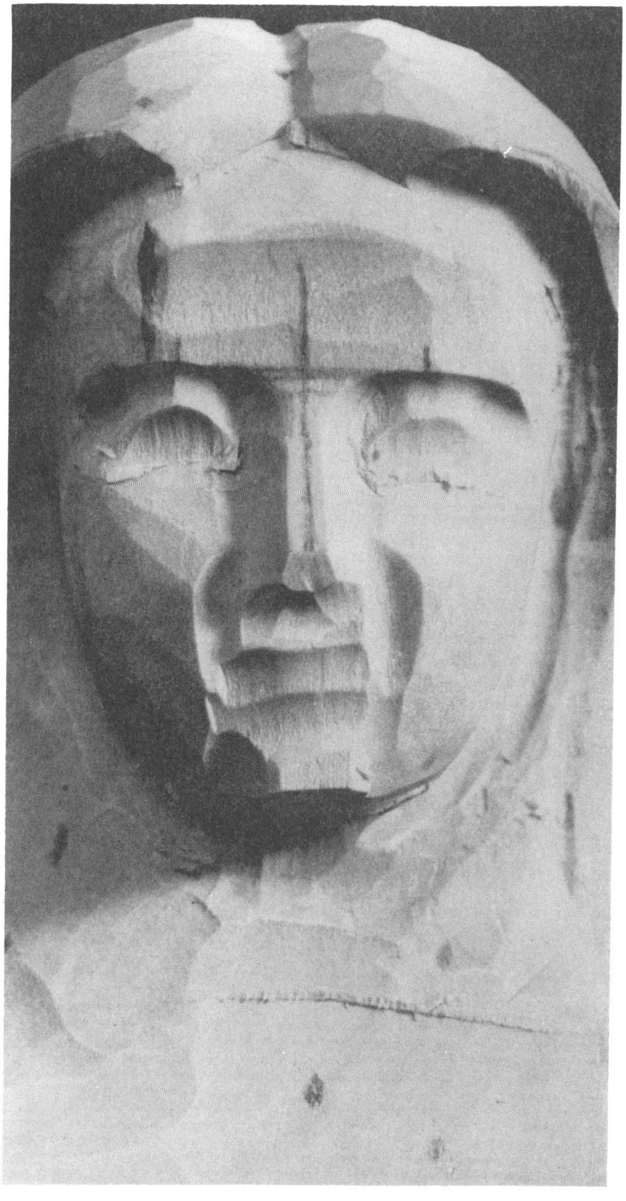

SECTION 5 SHAPING THE EYES

1. Outline the eyelid with a narrower #11 6-mm gouge cut.

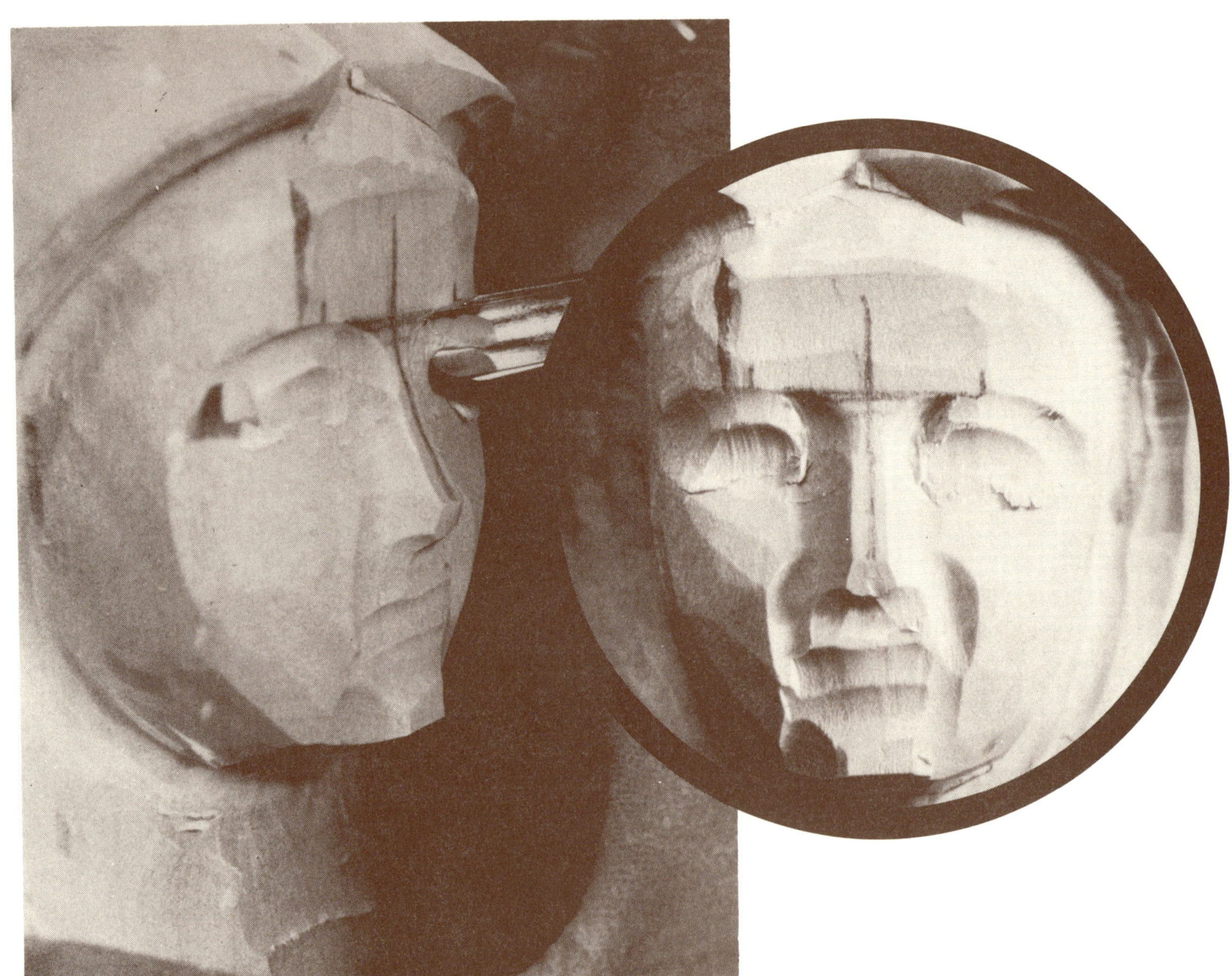

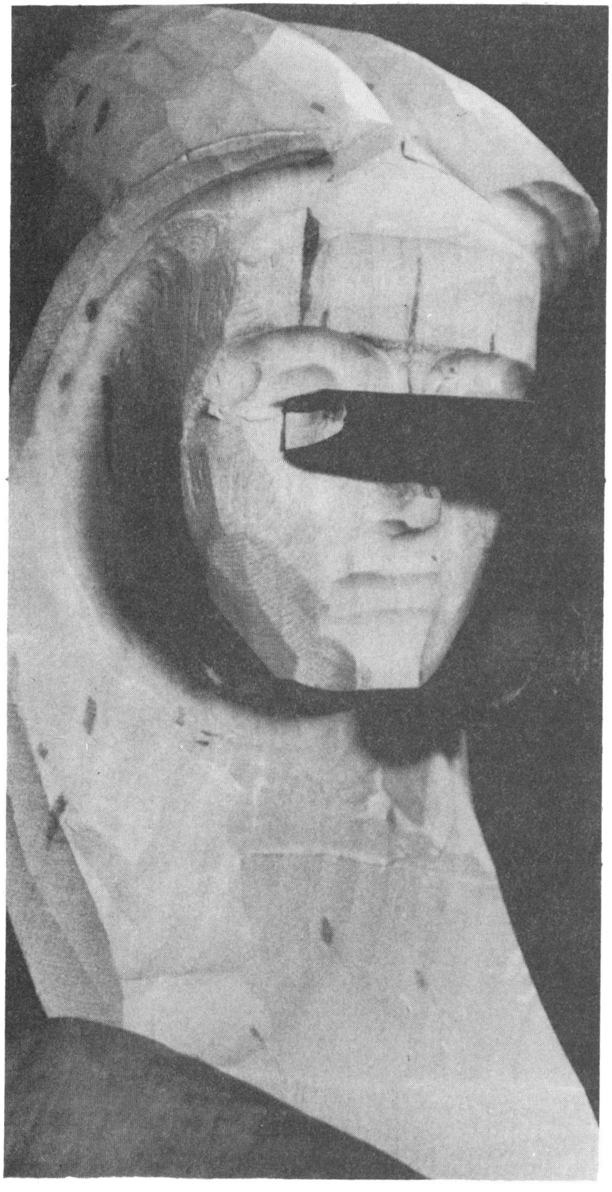

2. Deepen the corners of the eyes by 1/16" on either side of the bridge of the nose. ▼

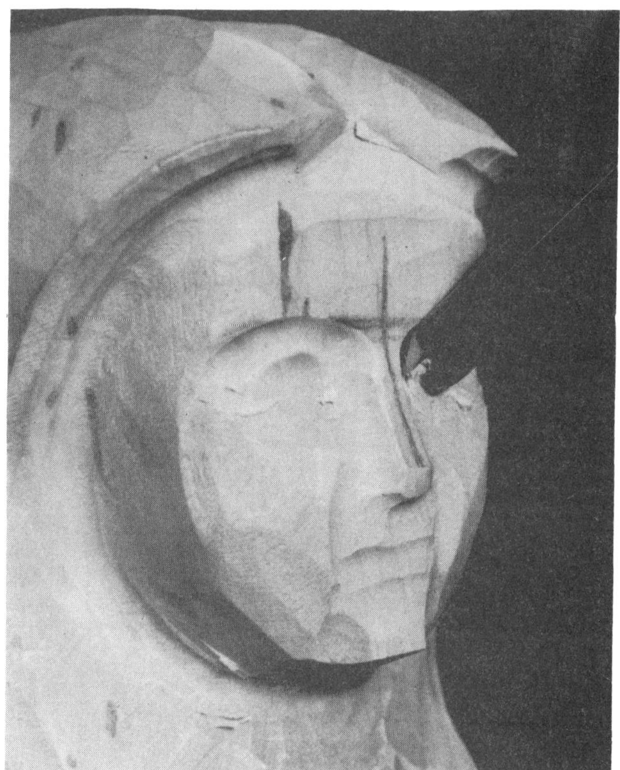

3. Using the same tool, define the bottom of the eyes, allowing approximately 3/16" for the eyeball. ◄

4. Using a small #11 1-mm gouge, outline the upper part of the eyelid. Begin at the center of the eye and cut to the outside. Cut from the center inward to complete the eyelid.

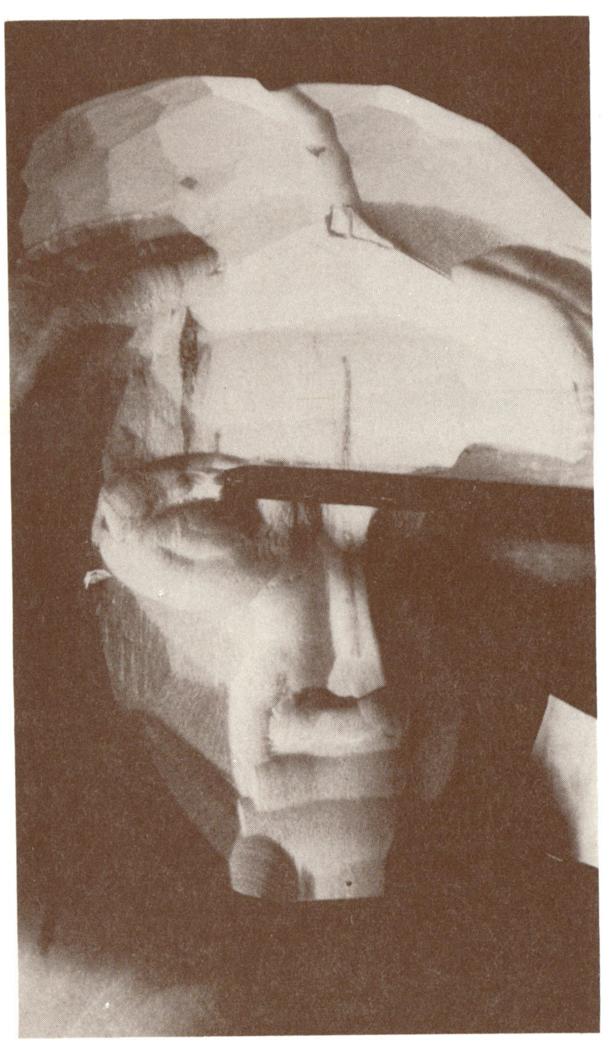

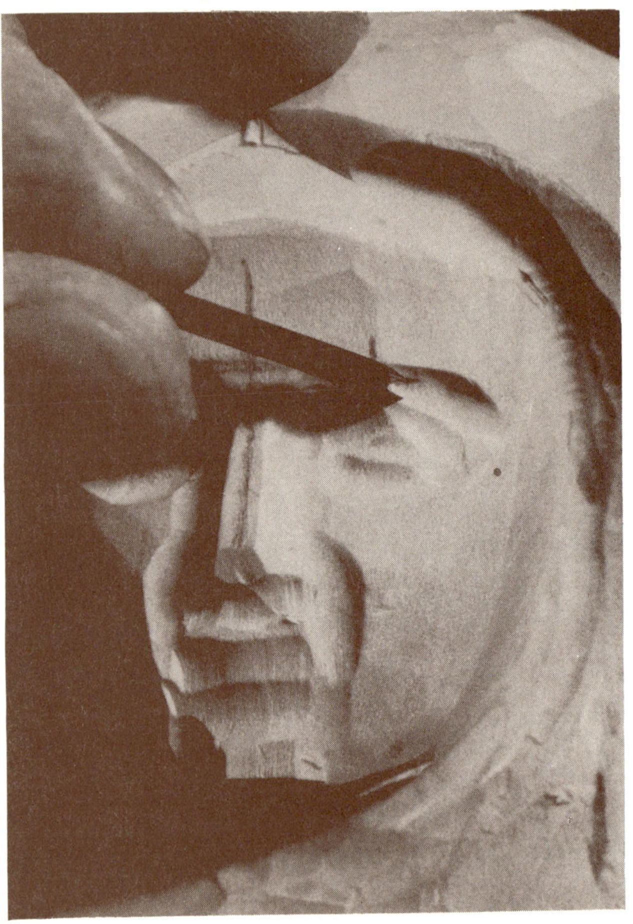

Repeat the process on the other eye.

5. Use a #1 6-mm chisel to cut back excess wood and shape the eyebrow.

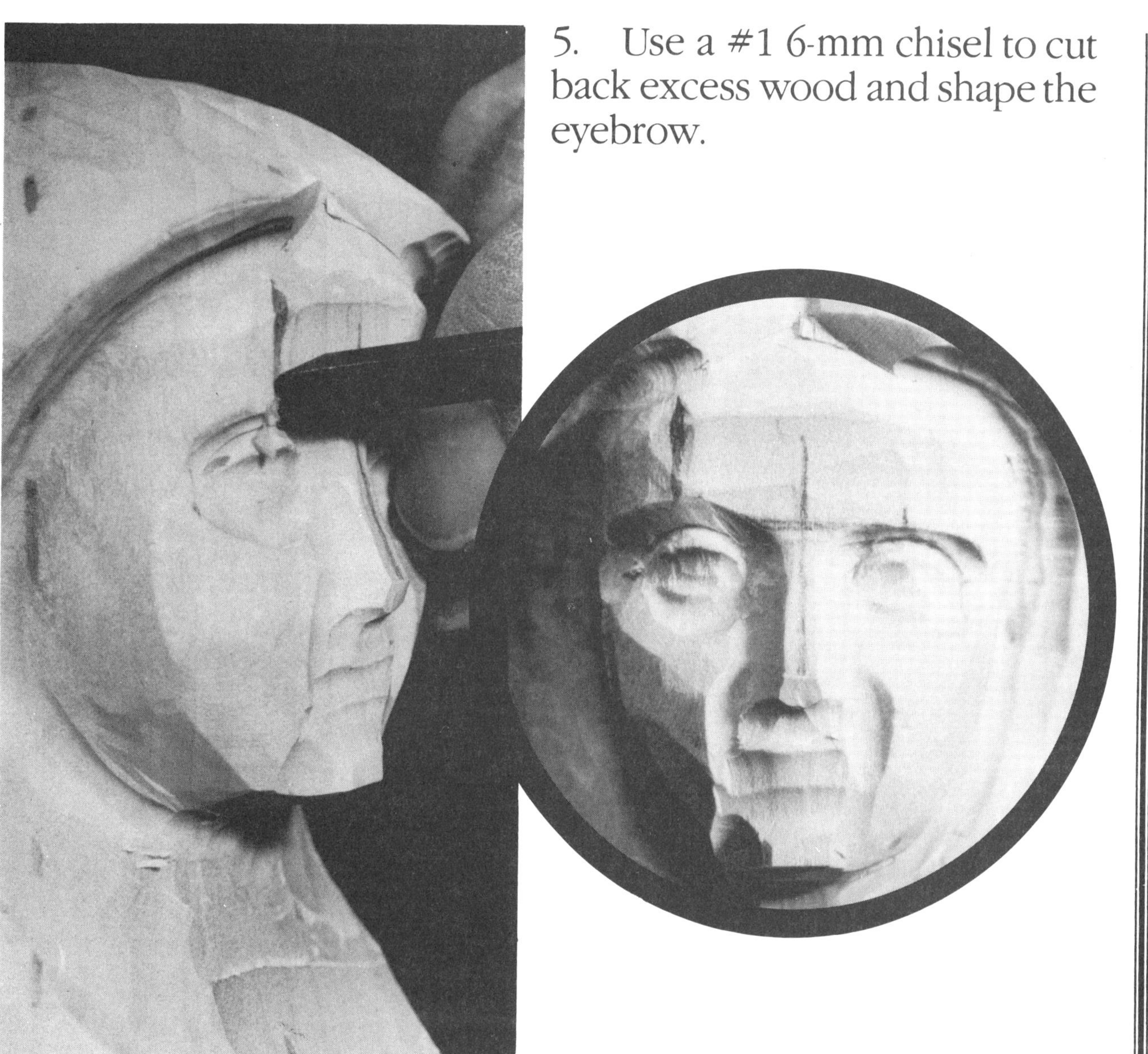

6. Using a #9 10-mm gouge, deepen the outer corner of the eyes to gain more depth.

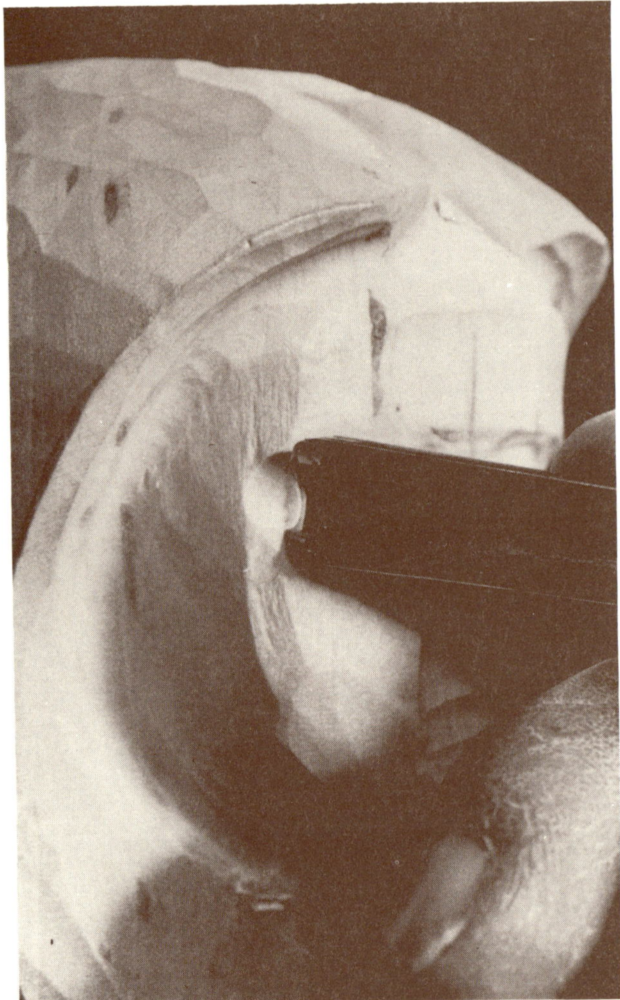

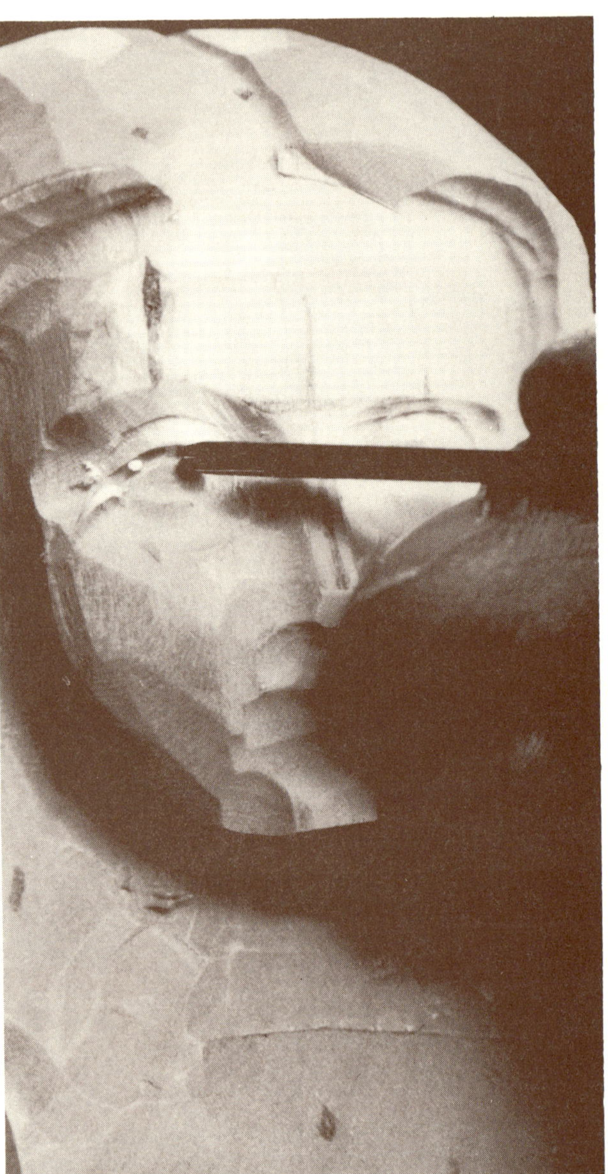

7. With a #11 1-mm gouge, cut the inside of the upper eyelid. ◄

Reverse the cut to complete. ◄

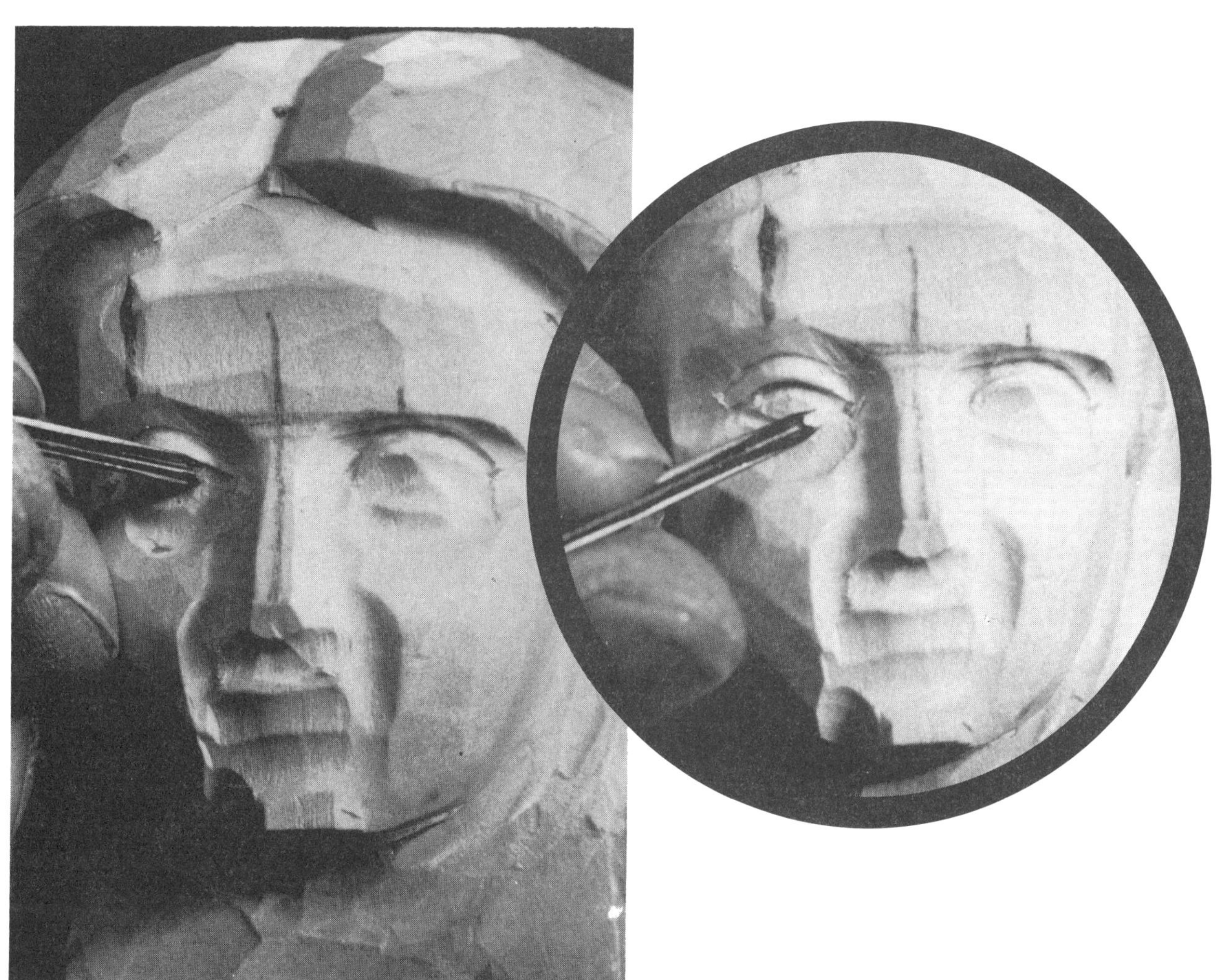

8. Using a #4 6-mm gouge, outline the lower inside of the eyelid. Work from the center of the eye to both corners. Repeat on the upper eyelid. ▼

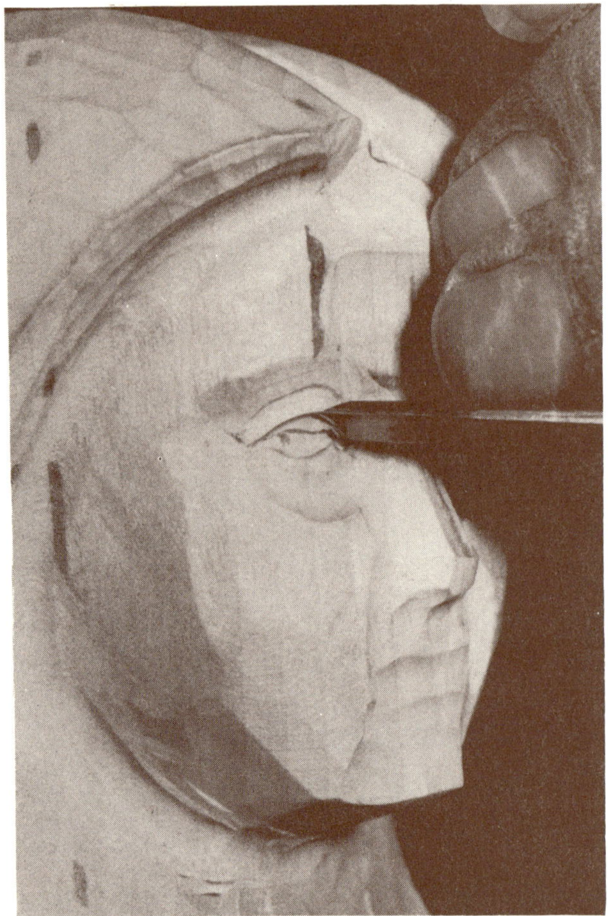

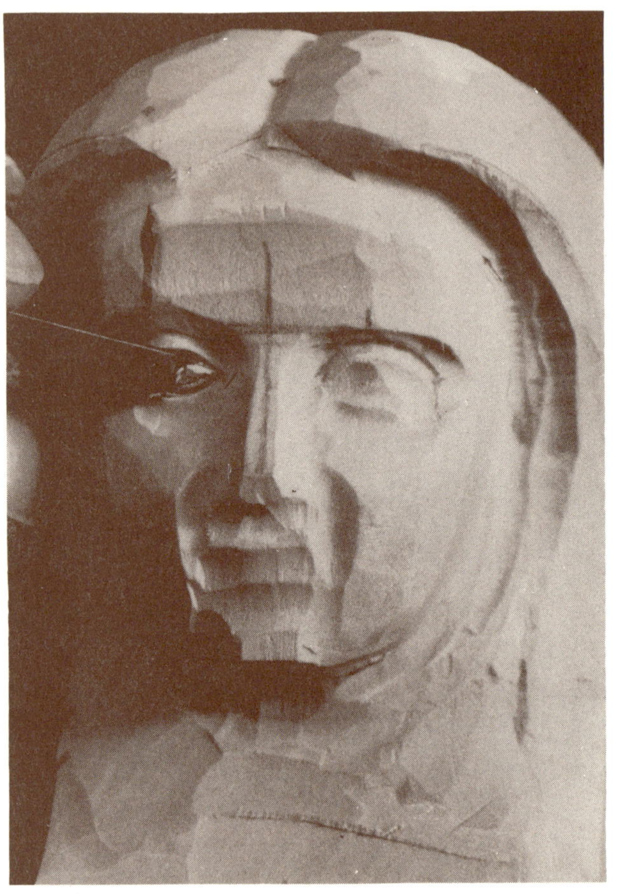

9. Clear and round out slightly the inside of the eyeball with a #2 4-mm skew. Complete the outside of the lower eyelid by defining it with a #11 2-mm gouge.

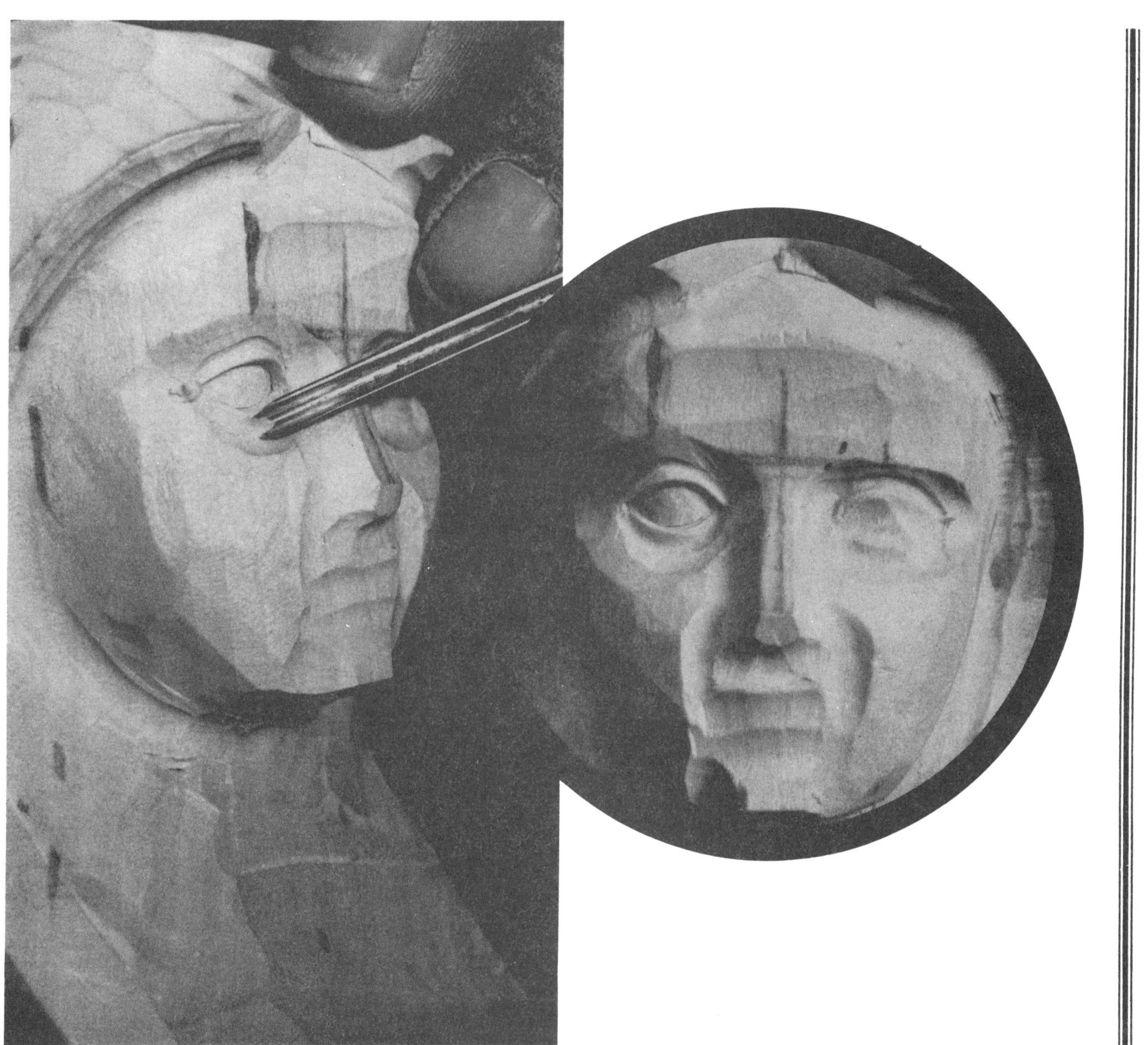

SECTION 6 SHAPING THE MOUTH

1. Cleanly cut the section between the upper lip and the nose. Outline the nostrils with a #11 1-mm gouge.

2. Define the center lip line of upper and lower lips by extending the cut to the corners of the mouth. Use a #4 4-mm gouge.

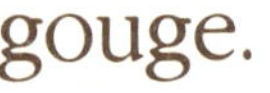

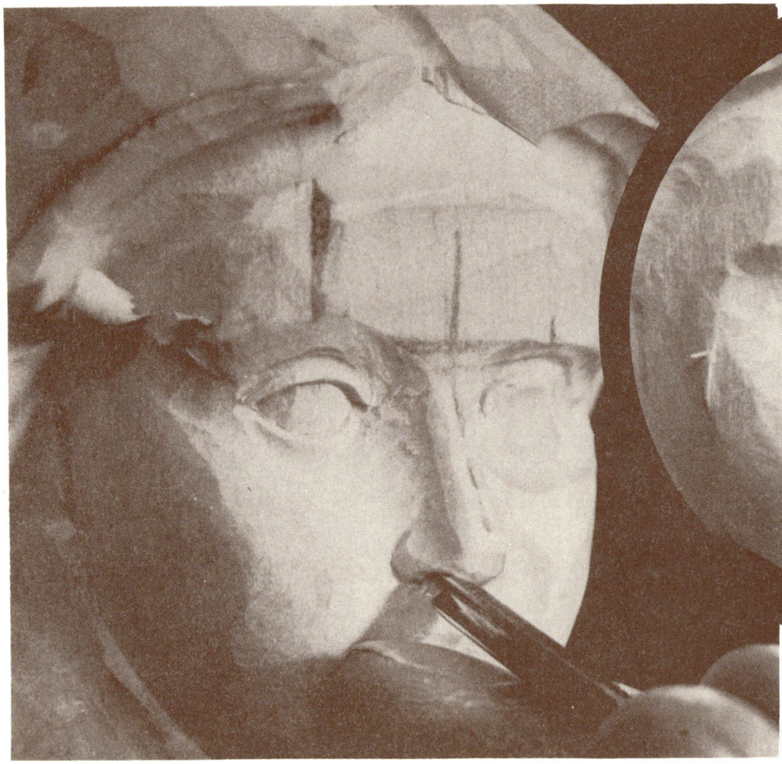

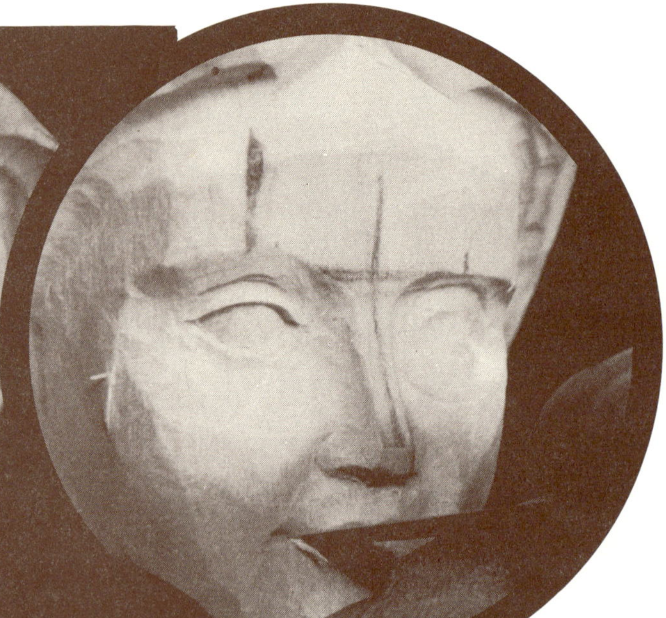

3. Shape the bottom lip using a #11 6-mm gouge by making a cross cut. ▼

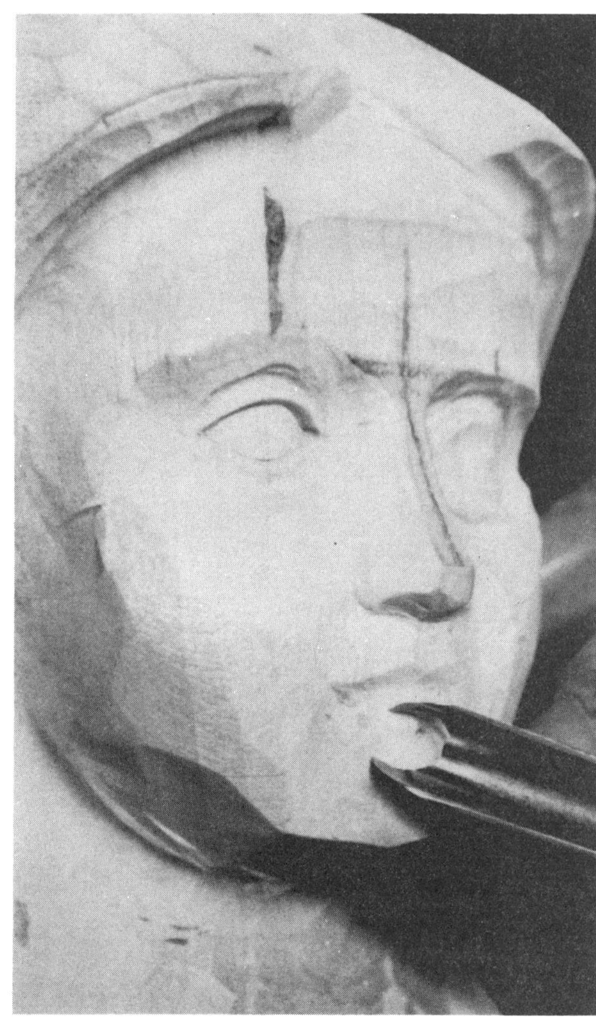

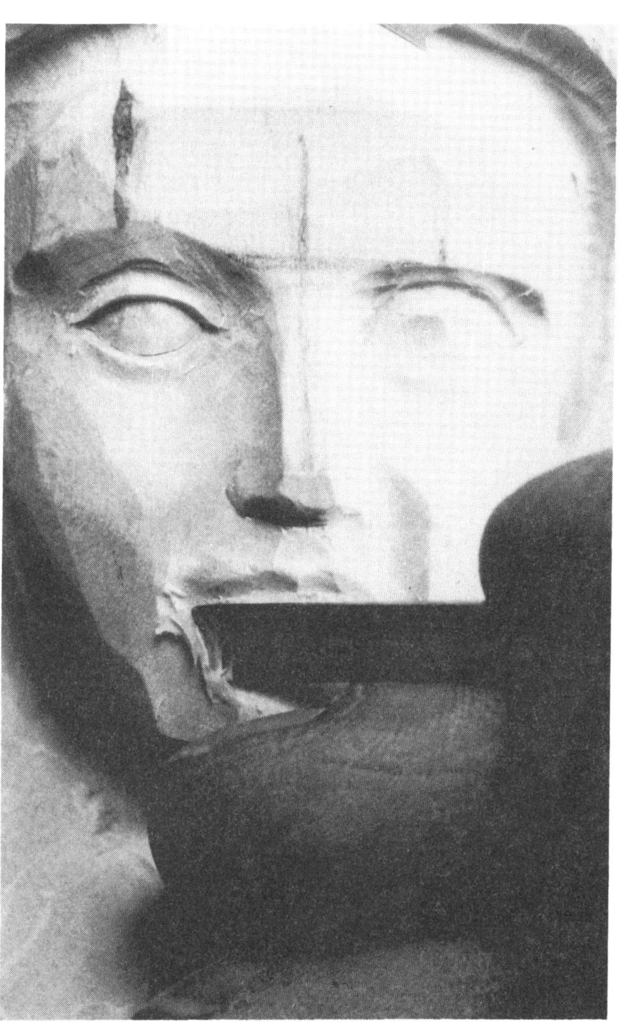

4. Remove excess wood from the bottom lip. ▲

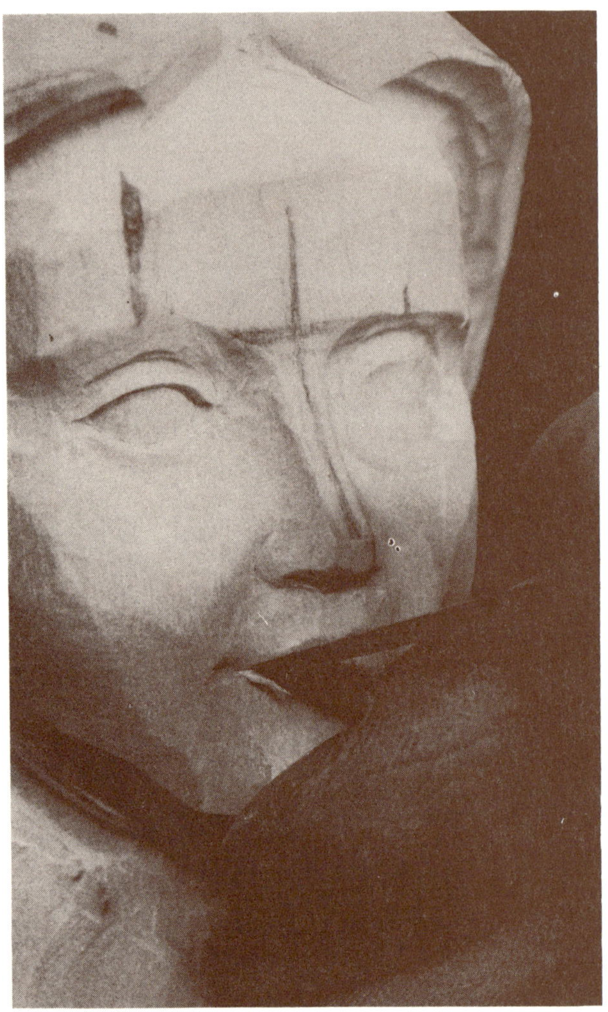

5. By using a #2 4-mm skew, define center lip line at the outer corners. ▲

6. Using a #11 6-mm gouge, hollow the outer corners of the top lip to create a smile. ▼

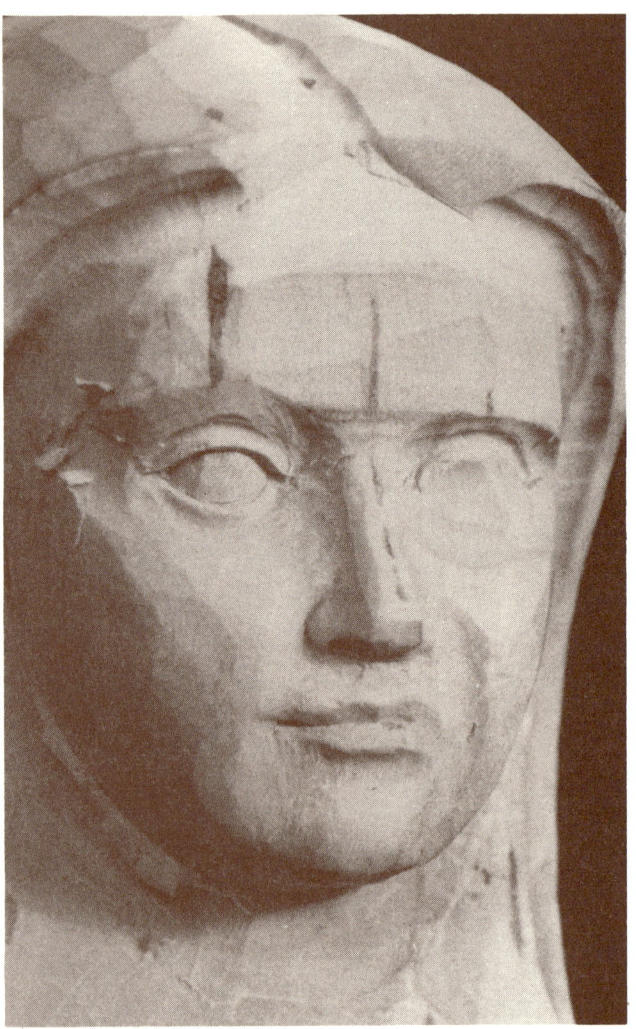

7. Use a #4 6-mm gouge to round off the chin.

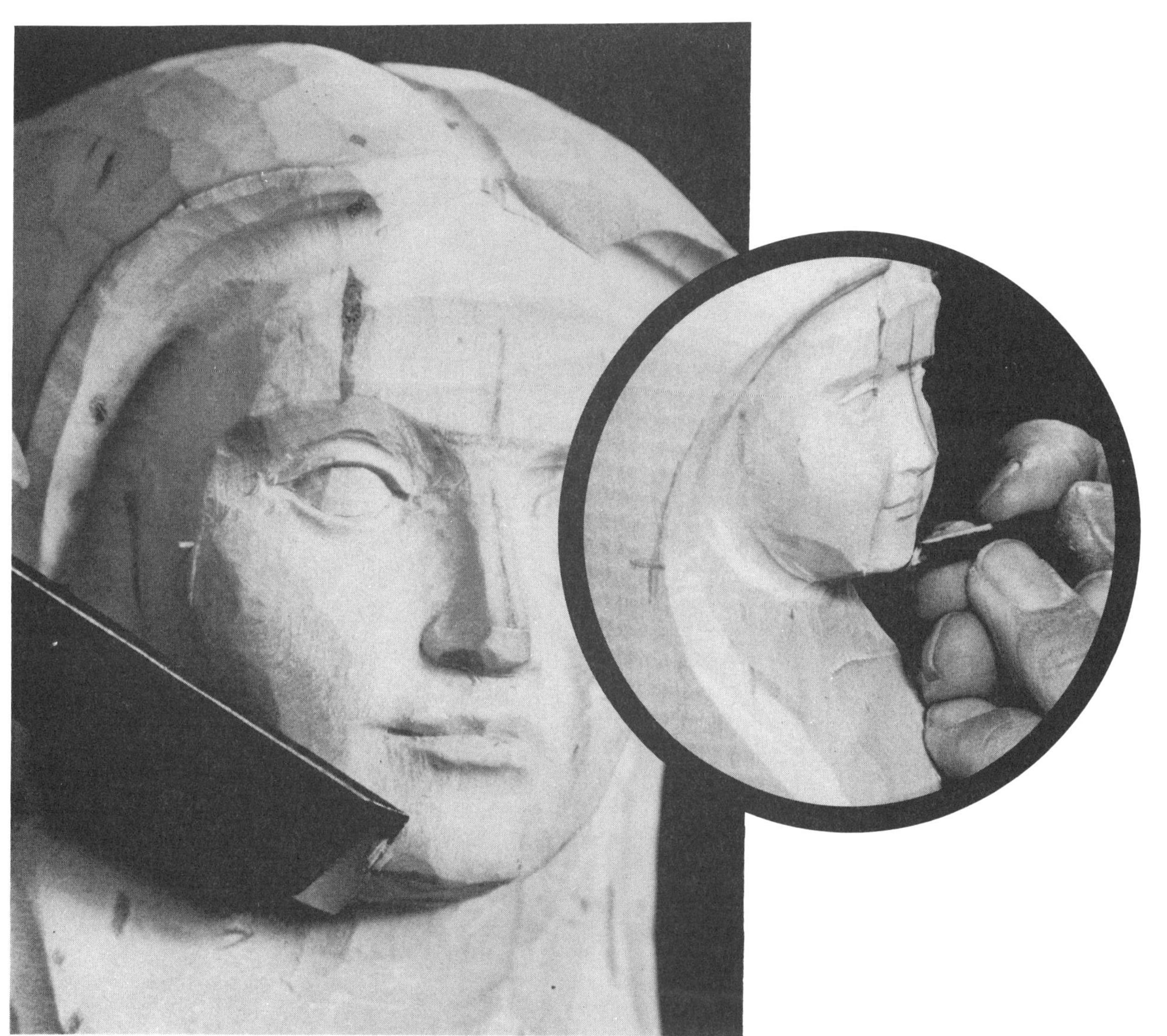

8. To smooth the cheeks, use a #1 12-mm chisel and finally a #2 ½ 18-mm shallow gouge, making small, clean cuts.

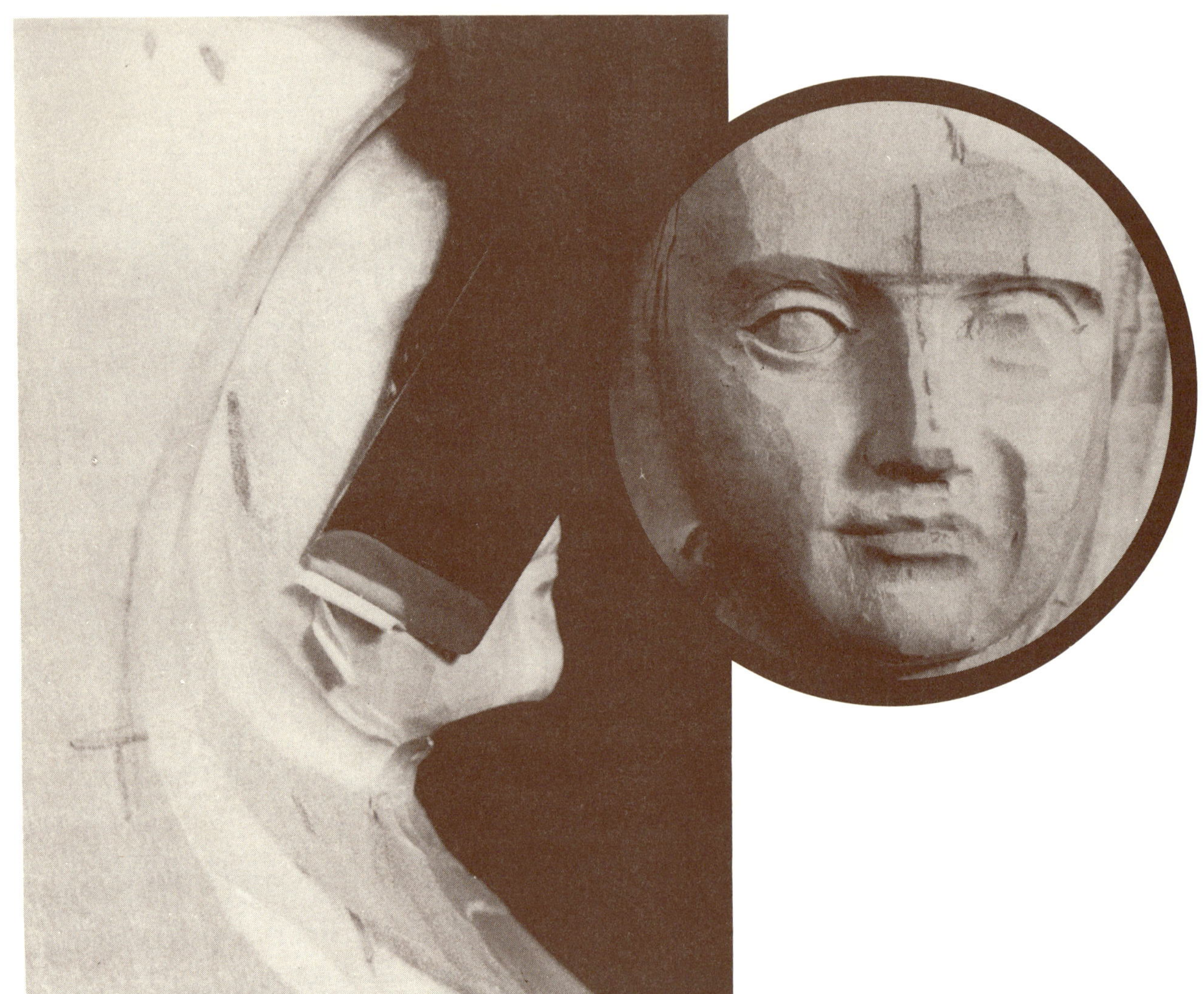

SECTION 7

FINISHING OFF

1. Using a #4 6-mm gouge, define cheek and temple area with a slight hollow at the sides of the eyes. ▼

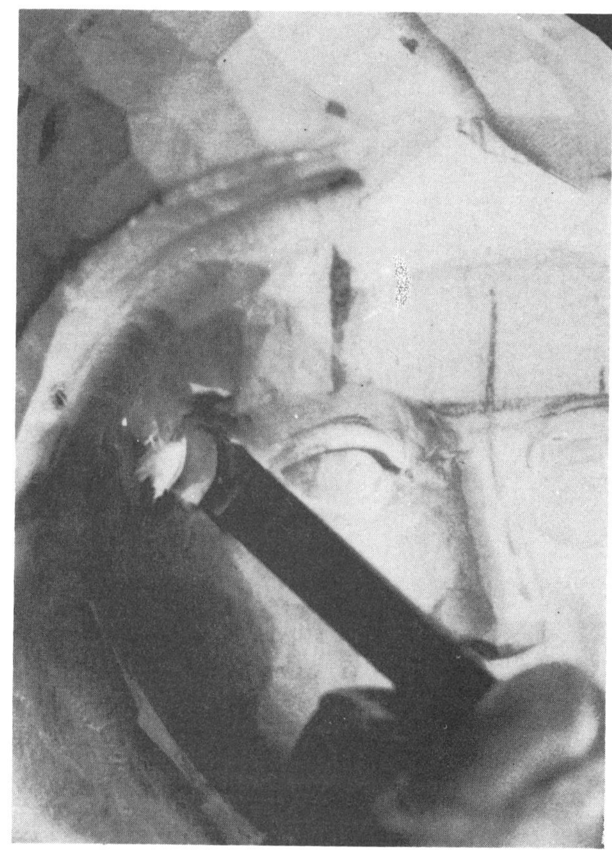

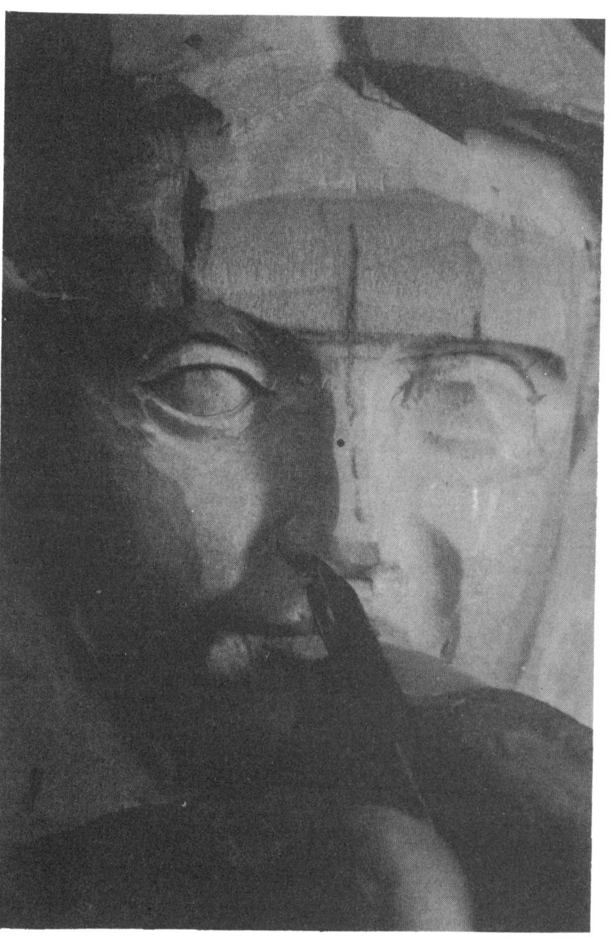

2. Use a #11 2-mm gouge to hollow out the nostrils slightly.

3. A #2 ½ 18-mm gouge is used to smooth out the bottom of the chin. ➤

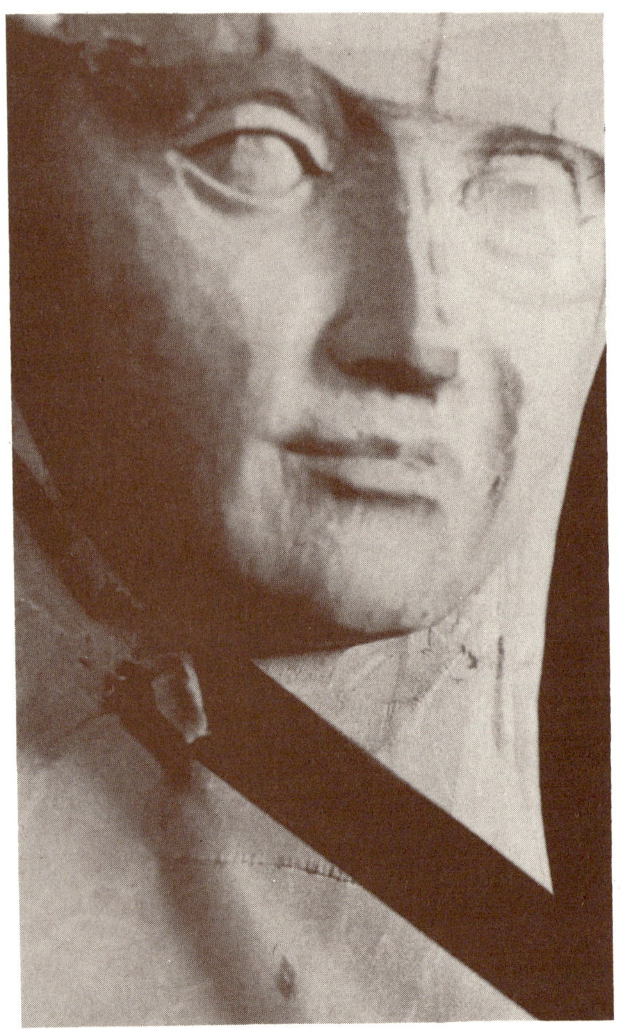

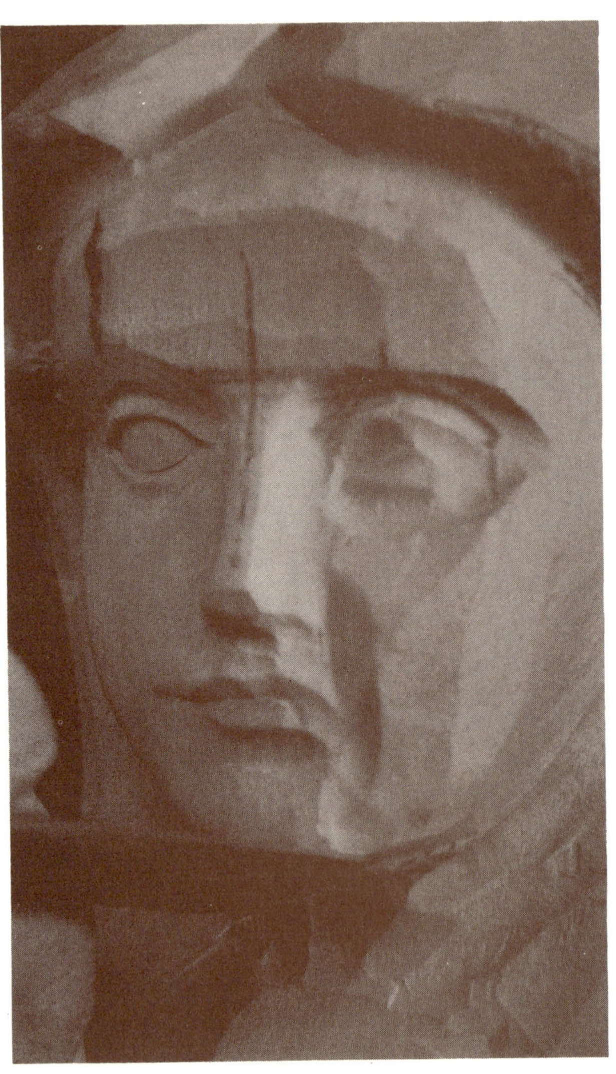

4. Clean the neck area with a #11 6-mm gouge. ◄

5. Use a #4 10-mm gouge to open the neck area. ➤

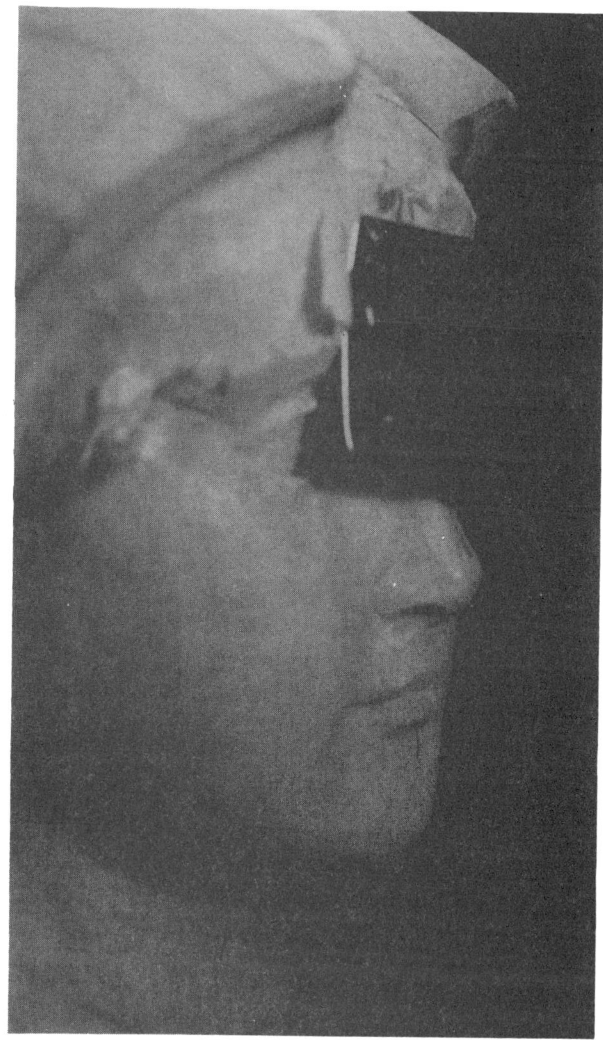

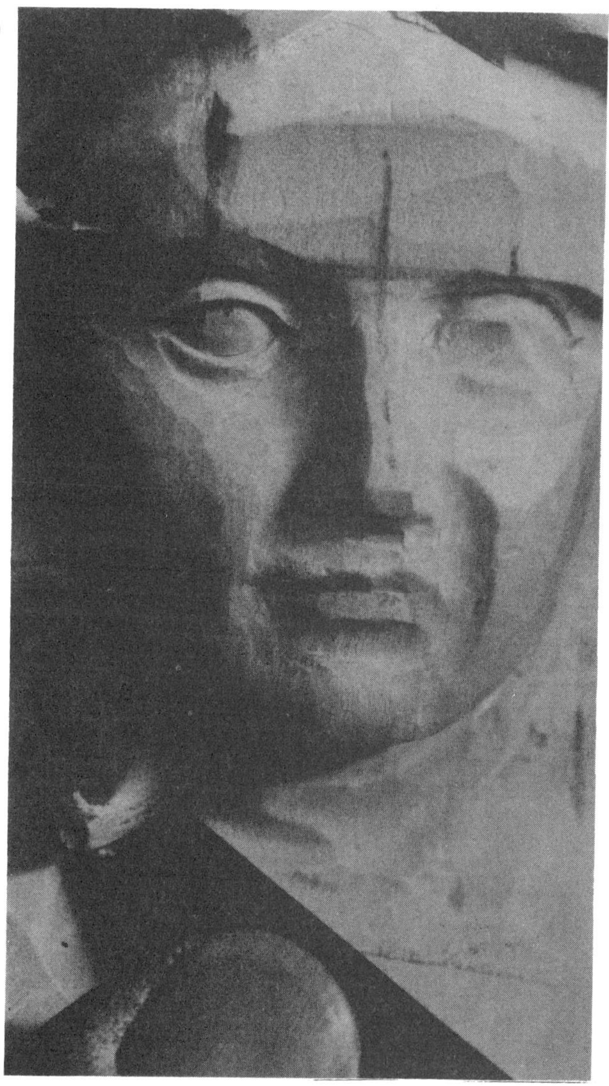

6. A #2 ½ 18-mm gouge is used to smooth the forehead. ◄

Outline the hair as shown. ▼

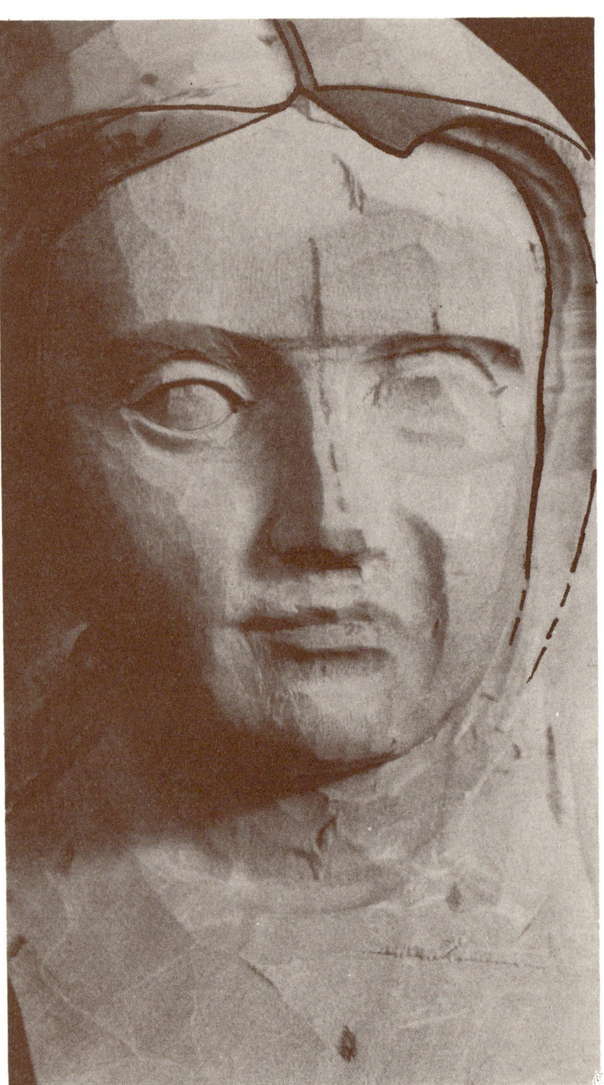

7. To create flowing hair, remove excess wood with a #6 18-mm gouge for the concave cuts and use the inside of a #2 ½ to smooth the outside.

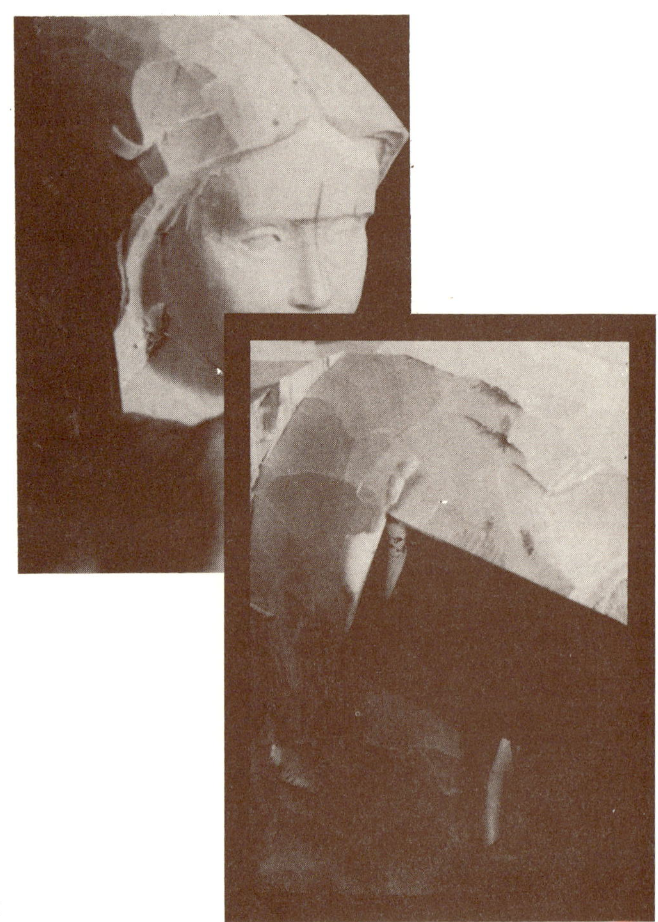

8. Use a #2 ½ 18-mm to clean the front edge of the hair. Use a natural wavy motion.

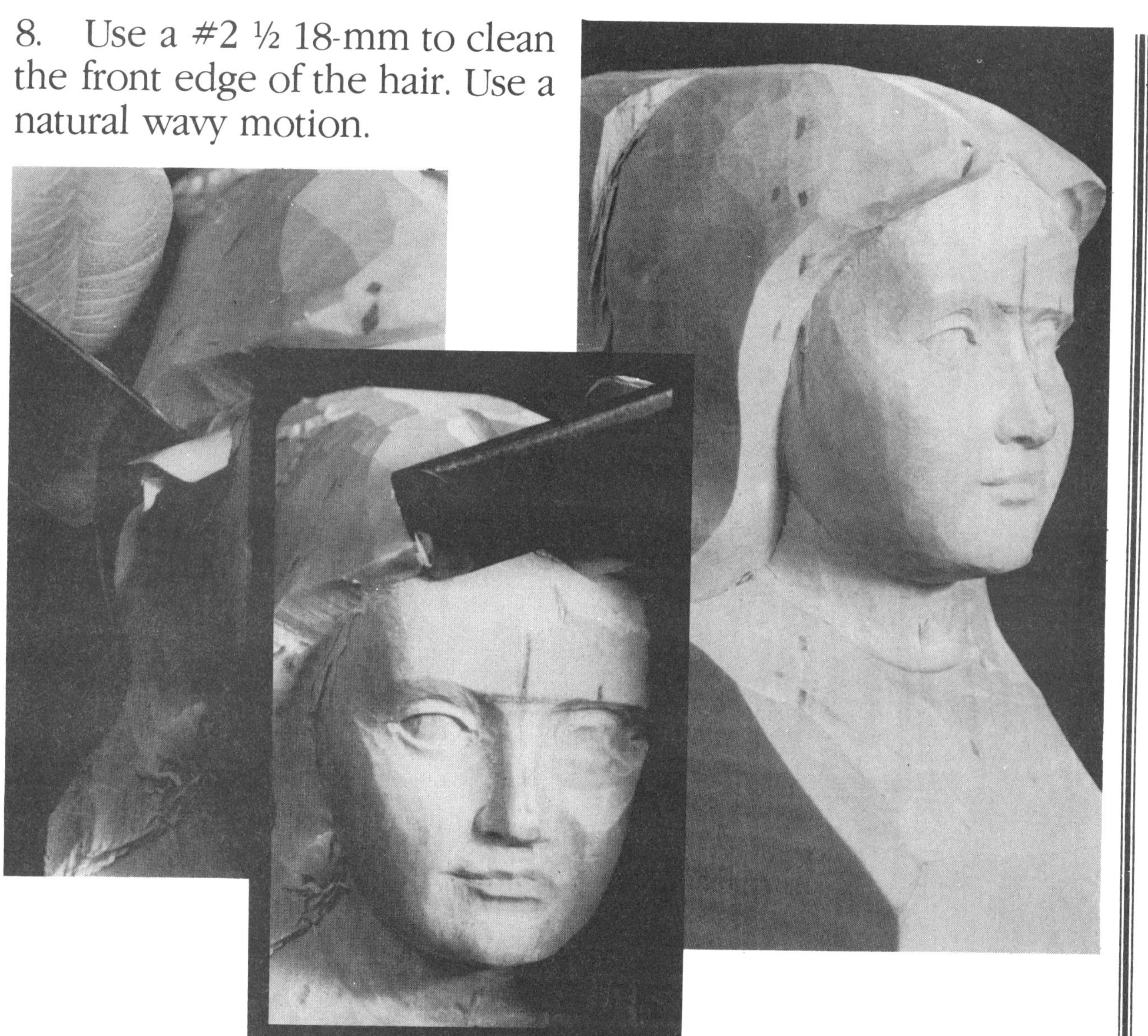

9. Using a #11 4-mm gouge, indicate hair flow lines.

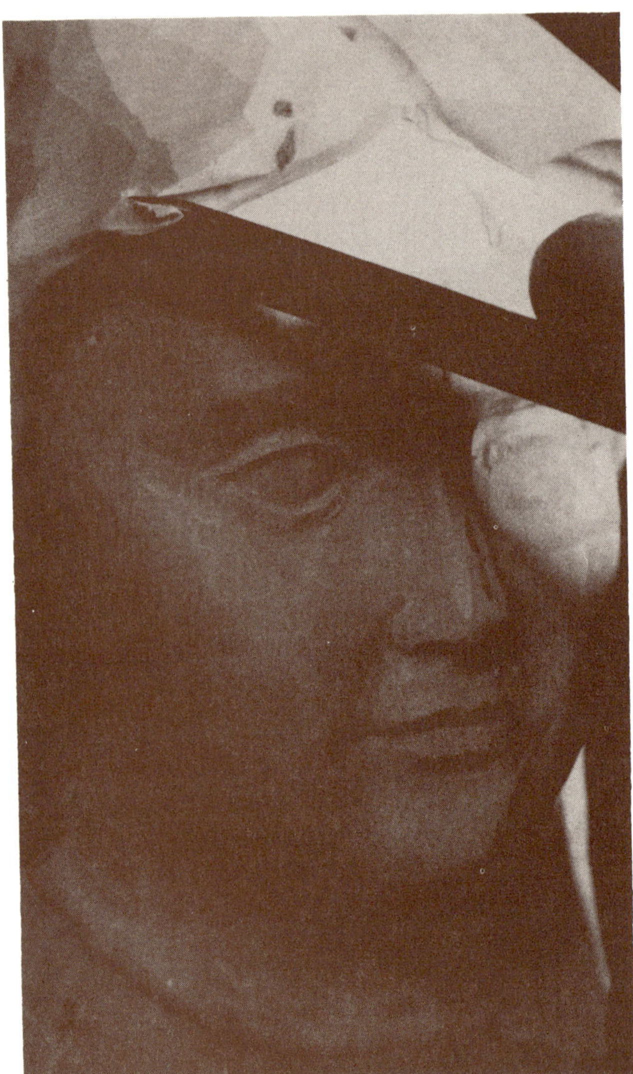

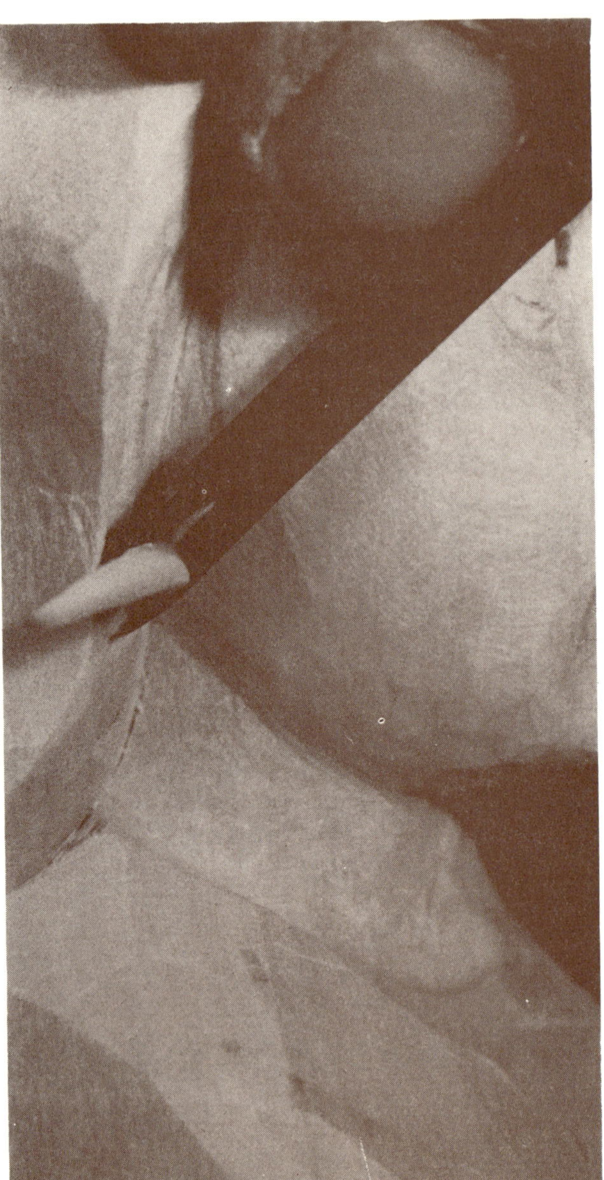

10. A #32 4-mm bent gouge will enable you to carve from the inside outward near the neck.

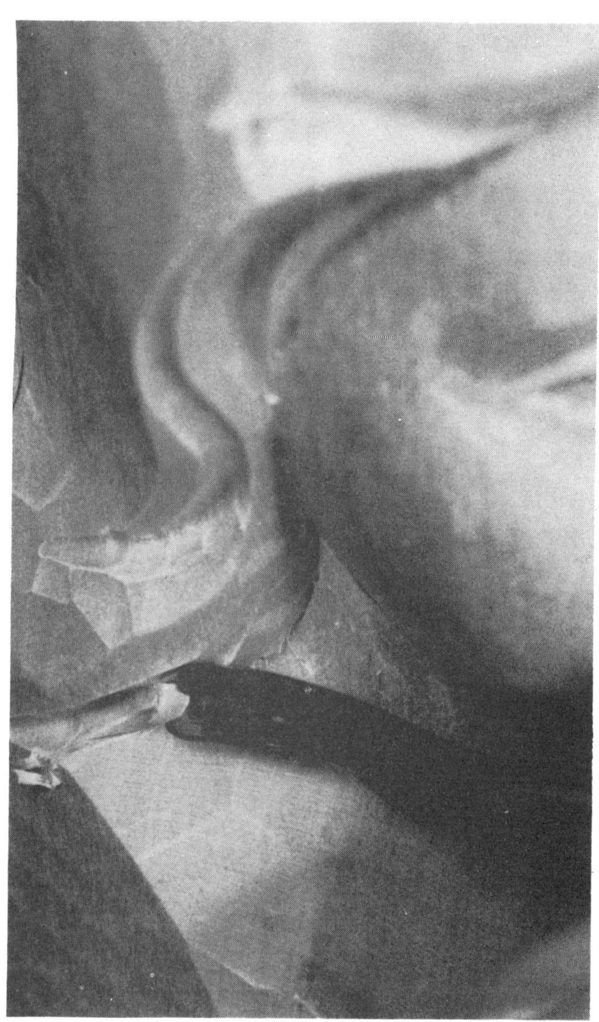

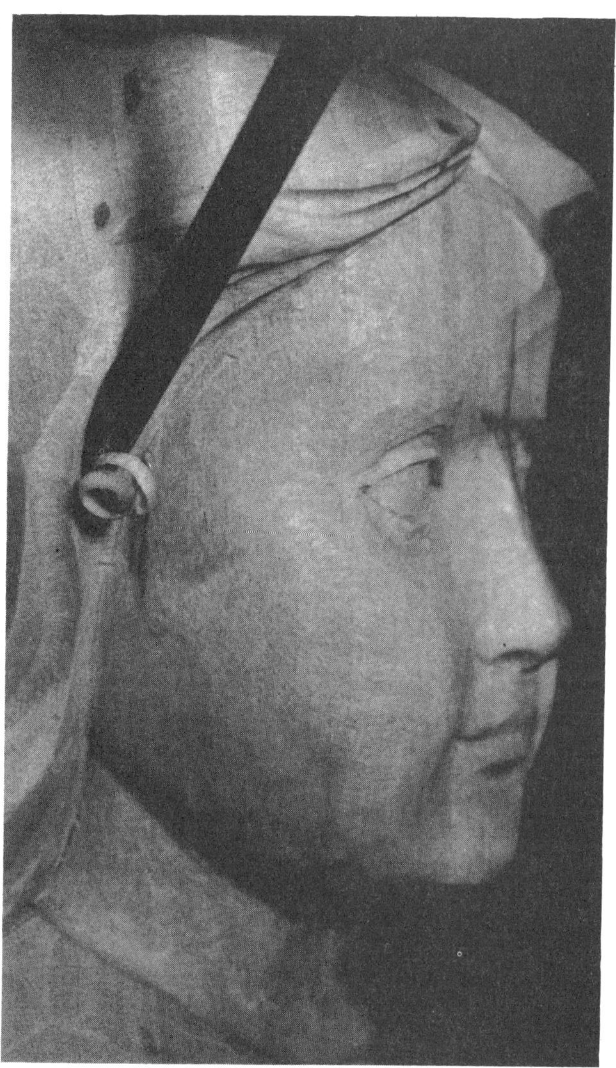

11. Use a #11 2-mm gouge for finer hair definition.▲

12. Use a #11 1-mm gouge for even finer hair lines.

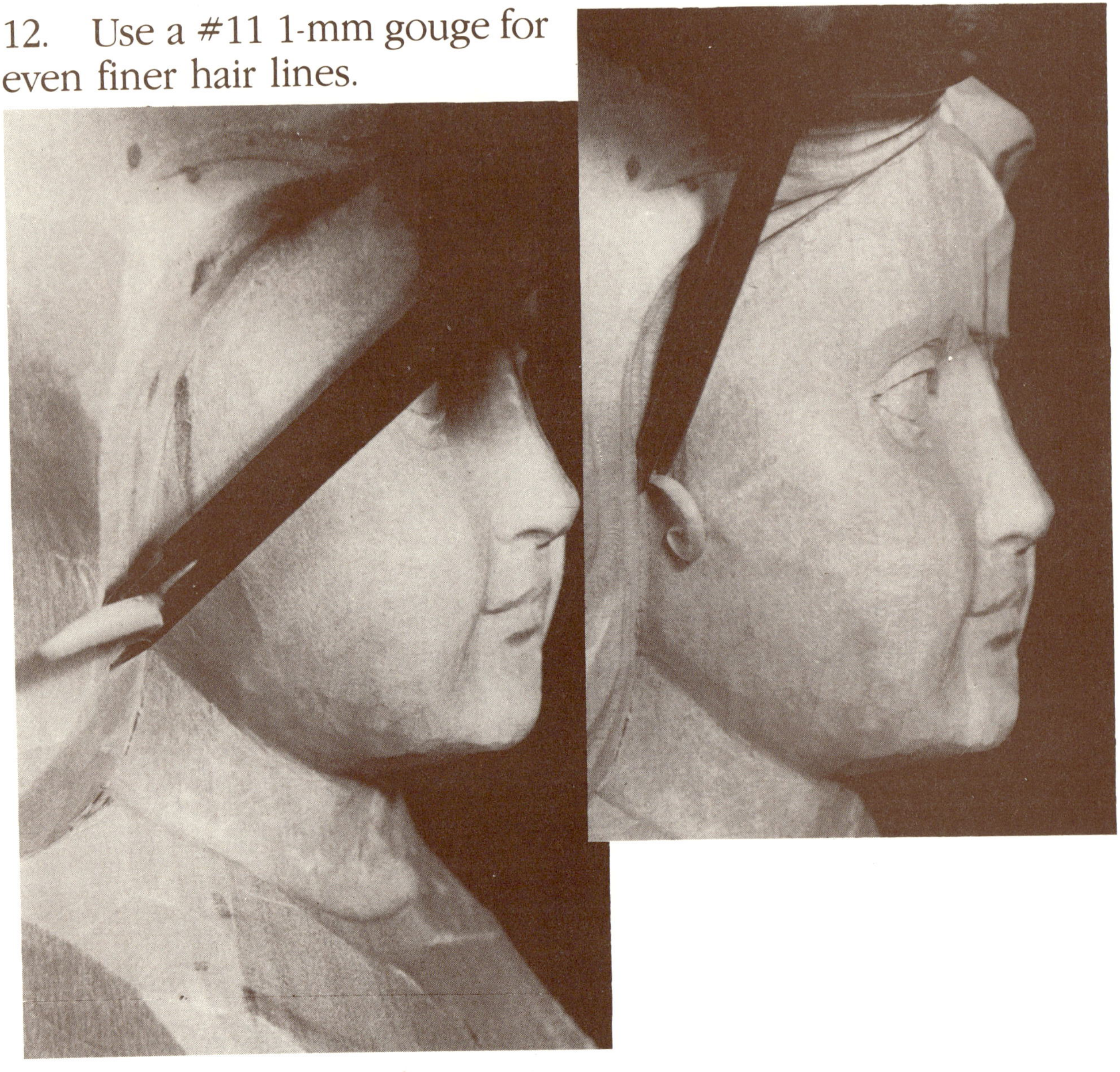

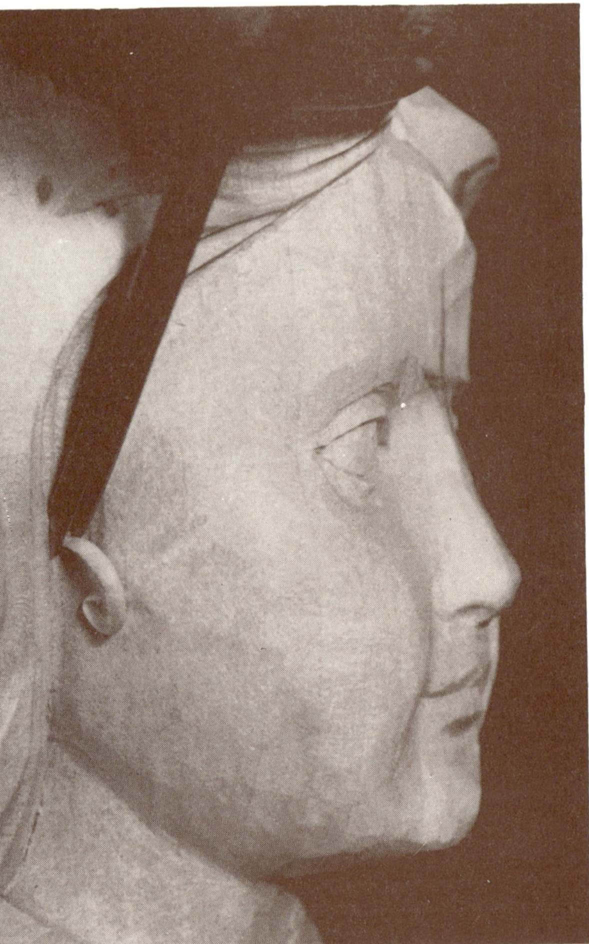

13. Shape the back of the head using a #2 ½ 18-mm shallow gouge.

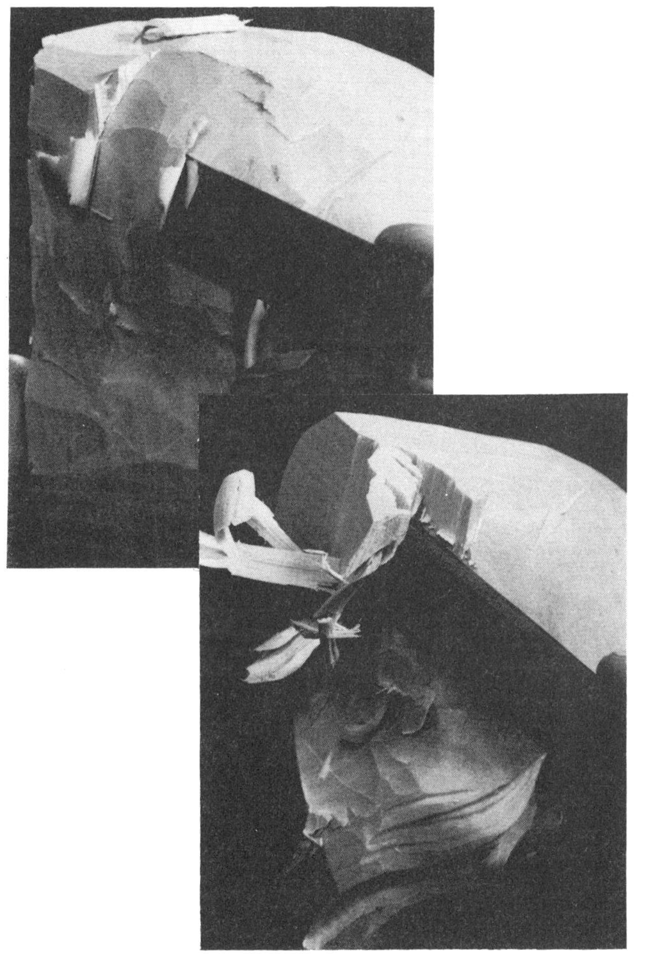

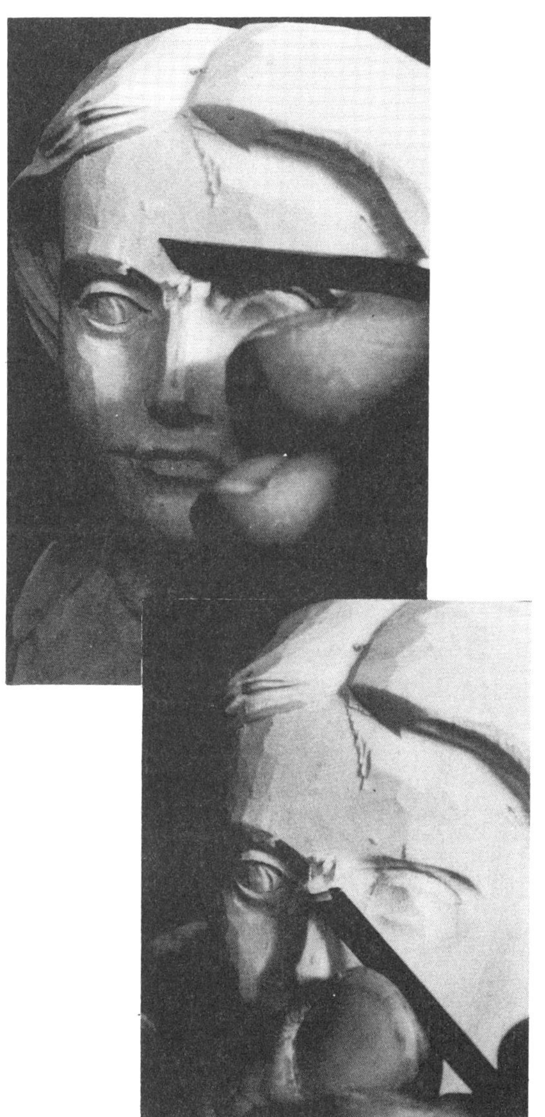

14. Use a #2 16-mm skew for cleanup work.

15. To complete your carving, more hair lines may be added as desired.

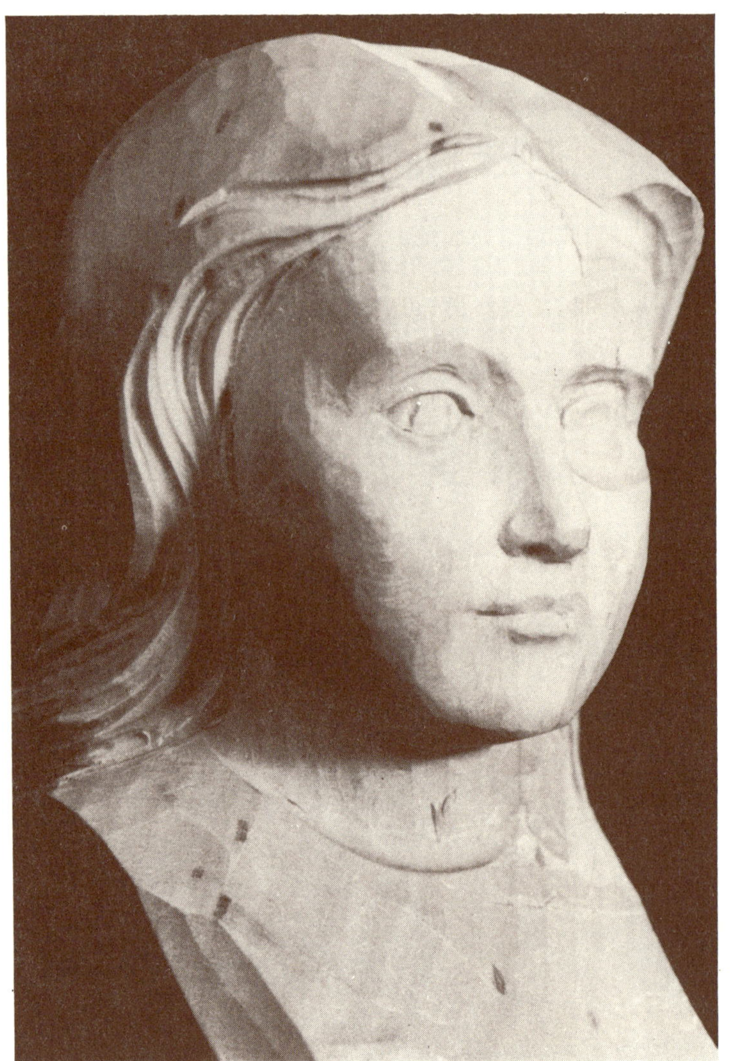

THE REST
IS UP TO YOU!

We hope this book has been helpful in learning to carve the female head.

GEORG KEILHOFER

Georg J. Keilhofer is a master woodcarver who studied his trade for eight years at the Schnitzschule in his home town of Brechtesgaden, Germany. During these years, some of his studies included freehand drawing, artistic lettering, clay modeling, history of art, cabinet making and, of course, sculpturing and woodcarving. Georg worked as a master carver in Munich and Brechtesgaden, Germany, before coming to the United States in 1966 with an exhibition of his woodcarving as a temporary feature at the Bavarian Festival in Frankenmuth, Michigan.

Since that time, he and his vivacious wife Anni have operated the Frankenmuth Woodcarving Studio. Georg has earned international recognition as a master woodcarver and teacher.